WHAT COLOUR ARE YOU?

Describes the physical and mental effects of colour and
how colour therapy can be combined with simple yoga
exercises to bring about a complete reorientation of body
and mind.

WHAT COLOUR ARE YOU?

THE WAY TO HEALTH THROUGH COLOUR
LILLA BEK AND ANNIE WILSON

Aquarian/Thorsons
An Imprint of HarperCollinsPublishers

The Aquarian Press
An Imprint of HarperCollins*Publishers*
77–85 Fulham Palace Road,
Hammersmith, London W6 8JB.

First published 1981
This edition published by The Aquarian Press 1987
7 9 10 8

A catalogue record for this book
is available from the British Library

ISBN 0 85030 616 7

Printed in Great Britain by
HarperCollins Manufacturing, Glasgow

CONTENTS

Life, like a dome of many-coloured glass,
Stains the white radiance of Eternity.
                                        Shelley

PREFACE

Ten years ago Lilla Bek decided to try yoga. She had heard that yoga could increase the circulation, quicken the metabolism and improve the organs of the body. It was good, they said, for improving the mind and memory and since she was not drawn to more athletic exercise, yoga seemed right. At least it was a little slower!

She suffered abominably. Although she had played regular sport before, she found her body would not bend in certain directions. The exercise brought on an extreme release of toxins, her head hurt more than ever and her body ached. To make things worse, although the relaxations at the end of each class were pleasant, she began to see continuous purple flashes in front of her eyes. With aching limbs and purples flashes she decided that next term she would take up flower-arranging! After the purple flashes came white ones – pure white light. She would open her eyes, presuming the curtains had been drawn because there was so much light in front of her eyes.

She persevered and the following term discovered with relief that she felt less dizzy when bending forward. The aches were diminishing and miraculously her bronchitis and poor breathing were also improving. She was, however, acquiring another kind of trouble! She was aware that something was awakening in her; her psyche was beginning to open. It was a gradual process but if, for example, she sat in a room she realised that the atmosphere around her seemed to lift and change. The energy field around her was changing its vibratory rate. The atmosphere was different; like a softer fabric on the cheeks.

Yoga had made her more sensitive to the atmosphere around her and she knew there was more to yoga than she had imagined. She began to know what someone would wear before she met them or when the telephone would ring. Just premonitions. Then a friend whose house was haunted invited her to visit. In one particular room was a bureau and when Lilla touched it she could feel the atmosphere changing.

There were more vibrations and she could feel these through the whole of her body.

She heard a voice in her head and realized it was her friend's dead father. When she finally allowed herself to listen he told her he had been strictly brought up in the Catholic church and could not go on to the next world without the final blessing of a Requiem Mass. When her friend arranged this there were no more ghostly visits.

From this moment Lilla began to open more and more. She was faced with the unusual and everything unusual fascinated her. She told herself that if she was going mad, it would be very interesting to watch as she went. She was not unduly perturbed or scared.

When she was alone, strange messages came through to her — usually when she was washing the dishes. She would find herself saying poetry she had never heard before or singing something she didn't know. Three doctors 'from the other side' gave her lectures on the evolution of man and how they would like her to use her reawakening abilities. They spoke to her before sleep, or when she was alone in the garden. She laughed and looked at it all.

Soon she was capable of all kinds of perception, including psychometry. Everything we touch becomes saturated with the substance of our being. Like a doctor who can tell our health pattern from a sample of our blood, Lilla could hold an object and have a very good idea of its history and what the person who owned it was like.

She discovered during one significant weekend that she had an affinity with nature spirits and tree spirits. She could 'speak' to them by tuning into the elemental world of images.

She would walk into places she had never been to before and see past events as though she had been there. It was as though she could project herself to places. During one particular week at Glastonbury, she caught a stomach bug and couldn't eat for days. She lived on glucose and water and realizes on reflection that she had in some way been put in the same position as ancient initiates — those people specially trained by masters to realize their full potential in body, mind and spirit. She was aware that her energies had been cleansed and were able to rise. She was ready for 'initiation'. It was during this time that she 'talked' to the spirit of Arthur and drew an impression of the first wattle church, an imprint of which she could see in the ether. A book that came later confirmed her vision.

It was comparatively late when she realized she could feel the quality of people's auras and the colours they transmit, and that by tuning into them she could tell a great deal about them. Interpretations of colours have evolved in the same way as astrological interpretations have evolved over thousands of years. Today, through the complexities of life, our energies acquire more complicated vibrations and Lilla's gift of understanding makes her aware of the wider implications.

It was not so much the physical side of yoga as much as the relaxations which had the deepest affect on her. But yoga, she began to know, is a key that opens the door to different types of consciousness, both inwardly and outwardly.

Lilla Bek has been teaching yoga for nine years. She has lectured around the country and taken part in workshops. She now spends her time giving readings on the chakras and past lives, where they relate to a person's present life and needs. She also takes part in research into the meaning of her gifts and is a consultant to the *Yoga Times*.

Annie Wilson is a journalist, researcher and writer with particular interest in new ways of understanding. Her first book *The Wise Virgin* shows how certain women have become catalysts in restoring the harmony between male and female energies.

INTRODUCTION

Every single surface in the whole world, whether mineral, plant, animal or man, is light sensitive. Take any metal and expose it to the sun, and it will tarnish in its own time. Some faster, some more slowly. Even gold, called precious because it does not tarnish, will take in a little, depending on the quality.

The skin of every living thing is aborbing light. However primitive the nervous system, any organism responds to light received on its surface. Without light there could be no life. Primitive man knew that and worshipped the sun as God.

Dr John N. Ott, America's leading light researcher, has also discovered that the eye has two separate functions. Light affects the optic nerve which enables us to see. But light also enters the normal eye and hits a special layer of cells in the retina which have no connection with vision. The light stimulates electrical impulses to the brain and some of these enter the hypothalamus, a nob about the size of a golf ball that sits at the base of the brain.

Research has shown that the hypothalamus plays an important part in regulating the most basic functions of our bodies. It controls the powerful pituitary, the endocrine or ductless gland that lies below it and referred to as the 'leader of the endocrine orchestra', which secretes important hormones into the blood stream. The hypothalamus tells the pituitary what orders to send to the lesser glands, the adrenals, the sex glands and the thyroid.

By taking in light via the eye and via the skin, we are subconsciously using it – wisely or otherwise. Light can have a profound influence on many aspects of our growth and health. Light is directing happenings deep within the body.

Goethe, whose research into colour is still unequalled, said that if we measure light and its interplay with darkness, the two extremes – light together with darkness – create a whole spectrum of colour. We live between darkness and light and this becomes a colour world. Colour is a property of light through its interaction with darkness.

Colour, then, is more than a decoration and a pleasure to the eye. It is light, broken down into wave lengths, into different vibratory rates. An object that absorbs all the light waves with none reflected back is called black. One that reflects all the light back is called white. We see red when sunlight hits an object that absorbs all the colours of the spectrum except red, which reflects back.

Every colour sends out a vibratory rate of either higher or lower vibrations that very quickly creates an experience of warmth or coolness. Red, the longest wave-length, has the slowest vibrational rate. Violet, the shortest wave-length, has the fastest vibrational rate. Contrary to what people would expect, the high frequency of the blue spectrum creates a cool experience and the low frequency of red creates a warm experience – a reversal that science cannot easily accept.

Theo Gimbel of Hygeia Studios in Gloucester, one of our leading light researchers, suggests that the density of red restricts its mobility and slows down its vibratory rate. Blue, on the other hand 'opens', giving a feeling of space. A recent experiment at the National Institute of Health in Washington, showed that under blue light amoeba showed a loose, open molecular structure, but moved into a tighter 'packing' under red light.

Through sensing these vibratory rates, blind people can be trained to 'see' colours. Indeed, a Russian housewife taught herself to distinguish colours by holding her hands over them, and there are now classes in Russia which teach eyeless sight to students. Some, says Lawrence Blair in his book *Rhythms of Vision*, find that their tongues, earlobes or tips of noses are more sensitive to colour than their fingers.

People also notice, he says, that colours produce specific sensations. That red burns, orange warms, yellow is barely warm; green is neutral, and violet cools while pinching. Colours also sting, bite, hit, press, pinch or blow on the hand.

We now know that the seven basic colours of the rainbow, the spectrum that makes up the white light we see, is only a small part of what is called the electro-magnetic spectrum. As Lawrence Blair writes: 'Light, heat and colour do not exist on their own. Energy of different wavelengths stream from the sun and other sources but little makes itself felt to human senses by reflecting off and interacting with matter.' Visible rays are only a small part of the energy source. There are unseen vibrations, unseen sources of energy below the infra red and beyond the ultra violet that affect us, and it is these areas of energy that psychics are touching when they 'see' or sense things of which most people are unaware.

As Theo Gimbel says, what most of us see is the small area of the spectrum of colour that we are educated in this century to be comfortable with. But through the deep dark blues and violets which we cannot normally perceive there is rejuvenation, peace and tranquillity. On the other end of the pole we come to the shining, exciting, and vitalizing effect of reds, of which we cannot as yet conceive because they are too brilliant.

Most of us do not think about colour very much. We look at the paint on pictures or in choosing the colour for our car, but we have forgotten the fact that colour has a far more meaningful significance than simply an entertaining or decorative value.

The ancient civilizations of Egypt, Greece, China, Tibet, as well as the native American Indians who were more in contact with their bodies, had an inner knowing of the effects of colour. The ancient Egyptians, for example, had healing temples of colour and light. Or set aside special rooms as sanctuaries in which deep blue, violet and rose pink colours were used. Using these finer colours they could attune more peacefully into themselves.

Even in medieval Europe colour was thought to be one of the most important symbols in the world. Symbolic colours were fundamental to most of the religions of the Earth. When these people wore a colour it was not to look attractive but to attune to the divine spirits of the universe. And from these times, the Church has traditionally used different symbolic colours for ceremonial clothing. The religious colour purple, for example, combines the warmth of red with the coolness of blue to produce harmony and balance.

The ancients also recognized energies beyond those we normally see. All icons and religious paintings depict figures with haloes or radiating light energy around their heads. They saw these energies in terms of colour and yoga has evolved because it was seen that certain movements strengthened or depleted these energies.

There is a restriction put upon most of us not to be aware of colour; simply because we are not taught its wider implications. We learn that colour is a pretty thing without any kind of organization. There is no attachment to it other than its attractiveness.

When Cézanne and Monet, and also Kandinski, began to use colour in a way that people began to be aware of, there was a dawning of colour consciousness. Colour was not yet meaningful, but once people observed that a cow should not be blue and that this changed the atmosphere of a painting, questions began to be asked. Musicians, too, began to be aware that colour linked to music had a psychological impact on people. To light or paint a room was to experience the music differently.

In fact we do recognize colour all the time. We accept without thinking that colours have qualities, as phrases in our language indicate. We are aware that colour has emotional aspects when we talk of 'seeing red', 'feeling blue', being 'in the pink', and experience 'golden moments'. If we walk into a room where a quarrel has taken place we sense the air is heavy and sticky and 'red'.

Yet many experts who are aware of the impact of colour still only accept its psychological significance – for example, Robert M. Gerard, who in 1932 used coloured lights on prisoners and found that red excited them while blue calmed.

But at Hygeia Studios, Theo Gimbel has gone further into the significance of colour and into the deeper dimensions of colour, shape and sound. He feels that colour has a physiological effect on the body, as well as exciting the emotions. He correlates colour with shape and has proved that certain 'sacred' shapes combined with colours amplify the effect.

His work has led to the establishment of a consultancy to design various hospitals and sanatoria, combining shape and colour to benefit certain ailments or general well-being. Asthma, tension and insomnia have all been helped by the blue spectrum (violet, blue, turquoise). Lethargy and lack of vitality have been helped by the red, orange, and yellow spectrum.

Most allopathic medicines tend to paralyse the nervous system in one particular area to 'silence' the pain. This is not a cure, simply a removal of the symptoms. But many doctors are now aware of this, says Theo Gimbel, especially in America and Germany and colour, he feels, should be used as an auxilliary to medical treatment, not a replacement.

Alexander Schauss, director of the Institute for Biosocial Research in Tacoma, Washington, has recently reported that aggressive, hostile and anxiety-ridden behaviour can be suppressed in minutes by exposure to a specific shade of pink. The sedating and muscle-relaxing effects of pink are now being tried for geriatrics, adolescent and family therapy, prison reform and business. Says Schauss, 'Even if a person tries to be aggressive or angry, he can't. The heart muscles can't race that fast. It's a tranquillizing colour that seems to sap your enegy. Even the colour-blind are tranquilized by pink rooms.'

Others too are using colour in a significant way. The Sunfield Children's Home at Stourbridge treats disturbed children through colour or chromotherapy. And at the Rudolf Steiner-inspired Waldorf Schools, class teachers paint classrooms to correspond with the 'soul mood' of the children at their particular stage of development. Thus the first year classroom is always red. The quality of red stands outward and forward, strong and clear, and this, they say, is what the six year old child is, and he responds to it. The colours change as the children grow.

Important too is that colour should not be static. At the Bristol Waldorf School, for example, the walls are sanded and curved so the colours move in different shades and shapes.

For the light of our own world is not static. From the moment we wake into the morning atmosphere of deep violet before it becomes light, our light is changing. The morning changes into the deep blue of indigo and before the sun rises the horizon becomes lighter blue. Then the world becomes green, although we don't realize that light has gradients because it is absorbed into a tremendous amount of brilliance. Towards the afternoon the light becomes yellow, which then changes into the oranges of joy in the evening: traditionally the time for singing and dancing. When the sun sets it can be a very beautiful red.

Our everyday world completes twenty-four hours as a spectrum of colour. The mobility of light is so fantastic that any static light is already an imposition on the energy of human beings. So we can see that as man moves towards an artificial, controlled environment and uses more man-made light sources, we are beginning to throw ourselves out of harmony.

As John Ott has realized, the shortage of natural light and the greater use of artificial light, creates more and more physical and mental disorders. We all know that strip lighting in a canteen can cause a nervous response to what we eat. And that candlelight produces calm and well-being. So far there is no artificial light that has all the properties of natural light, but we can begin to see that we need the impact of lights of exact quality of filter to keep our environment healthy.

We can begin to see, too, that since life begins with light and is sustained by light, our physical health and efficiency depends to a great extent on whether our colour balance is maintained. The vibratory value of colour can be used to restore our own vibrations, when through wrong living, thinking and feeling we become out of harmony.

This book, however, goes further — into the all-seeing eye of intuition and psychic awareness. We can begin to see that there is a connection between our physical eye and the third eye of the psyche; a connection between the skin and the aura; between the glandular system and the circulation of 'unseen' energies.

The symbol of that connection is COLOUR.

CHAPTER ONE

CHAKRA ENERGIES AND THE AURA

Everyone knows that the energy of a plant is created from the sun's light. That chlorophyll, the green pigment within the plant, draws energy from the sun to break down carbon dioxide, synthesize sugars and absorb them as food. But less understood is the device that human beings have for taking in and using energy. Energy that comes in not only from the sun, but from the rest of the cosmos. What is this receptivity in us? How do we receive the energy we need to survive? Do we have vital points in our body that receive, assimilate and transmit energies, and can these vital points diminish or increase our energies according to the way we live our lives?

According to Frank Waters, in his book *The Book of the Hopi*, the Hopi Indians of North America, who believe themselves to be the oldest inhabitants of that land, thought the human body and the body of the earth were made in the same way. Both had an axis: in man it was the spine, which controlled the balance of his movements and the functions of his body. And along this axis, they said, were several vibrating energy centres which would give a warning if anything went wrong.

The first centre, said the Hopi, lay at the top of the head. Here, when a child was born, was the soft spot, 'the open door' through which he received life and communicated with his creator. As the child breathed, the soft spot moved up and down with a gentle vibration that was communicated to the Creator. When 'Talawva' came, the 'red light' time, the last phase of creation, the soft spot hardened and the door closed. It stayed closed until his death, when it opened again for life to leave in the same way it had come.

Just below this was the second centre, and the organ with which man learned to think by himself: the brain. The third centre lay in the throat, linking the openings in his mouth and nose through which he inhaled the breath of life and the vibratory organs that let him give back the breath in sound. This primordial sound, like that which comes from the vibratory centres of the body of the earth, was tuned to the universal vibration of all creation.

The fourth centre was the heart. It, too, was a vibrating organ, pulsing with the vibration of life itself. If in his heart a man felt the good of life, its sincere purpose, he was of One Heart. But those who allowed bad feelings to come in were said to be of Two Hearts. The last of man's important centres, according to the Hopi, was under his navel, the area some people now call the solar plexus. As the name suggests, this was the throne in man of the Creator himself. From it He directed all the functions of man.

Tibetan and Hindu mystics, like the Hopi, put forward the idea of a similar series of centres of energy or force in the human body, as Frank Waters also points out. But they suggested that there were seven important centres, which corresponded roughly with physical centres of the body and they functioned psychically as well as physiologically.

Like the Hopi, they thought the highest centre was at the crown of the head. It was known in Eastern mysticism as the Sahasrara-Padma, or the thousand petalled lotus, and was associated with the pituitary gland of the brain. As the seat of psychic consciousness it was thought to be the most important centre and, as the Hopi believed, it was the door to the Creator through which consciousness enters and leaves. Below that, centred between the eyebrows, was the Ajna centre, which corresponded to the pineal gland, forming the basis of the brain and controlling the automatic nervous system. The Visuddha was the throat centre, made manifest in the thyroid and para-thyroid glands, and governed the lungs, bronchial and respiratory systems.

Below this, as the Hopi also said, is the Anahata or heart centre, corresponding to the physical body's thymus gland and controlling the heart, blood vessels and circulatory system. Then came the Manipura or solar plexus centre (the Hopi's throne of the creator), linked with the pancreas and stomach. The centre controlled the sympathetic nervous system which changed inorganic into organic substances and transmuted these into psychic energies.

Eastern mysticism, however, described two more centres below these which were not included by the Hopi. The Svadhisthana centre associated with the adrenal glands, concerned with the elimination of substances that cannot be assimilated. And the Muladhara or Root centre at the base of the spinal column which corresponded to the sacral plexus and represented reproduction.

When Lilla first began to open psychically she realized she could *see* these energies. We do have an 'etheric' body – a body of energy we cannot normally see. It is simply a different manifestation of energy from the seemingly solid energy we experience in everything we see around us. In fact it is a vehicle, a direct counterpart of the body, which reflects its inharmonies. It consists of rotating movements of energy or force and where these interweave more closely, these 'centres' produce a steady glow of colour.

There are actually quite a few of these centres of energy in the etheric body, but seers and clairvoyants − ancient and modern − generally agree that there are seven major centres or CHAKRAS. Even so, it is important to remember that seers themselves are all at different stages of development on different paths of discovery and will interpret what they 'see' accordingly.

Lilla's path at this moment lies within health through yoga and this is a book about what she sees and how she interprets it. It is a book about health and about the body, for it is the body which maintains the balance in all areas of our lives − physical, emotional, mental and spiritual. And all these levels of life are reflected in our chakras. It is a book about how the state of our chakras makes us what we are at any one moment and how that state can change.

Only gradually, as Lilla became more aware of these energies, did she see that each centre had a particular colour. Quite often she would notice in a yoga class that someone was extremely yellow or red or blue. Just by looking at them she could feel in which centre their energies were depleted or over-charged. And while most of us have hunches when a friend is unwell, not quite healthily balanced even though they look all right, Lilla could go further. She could sense that someone had too much energy at the top of their body or too little below the waist. She could feel the patterns of energy flowing around the body and could tell where there was too much or too little.

Things not seen are difficult to comprehend, so it is necessary to explain a little more about the chakras. These force centres, these fine threads of energy, are focal points which receive energies to vitalize the physical body. Chakra means circle, and chakras are like three-dimensional pulsating wheels that rotate rhythmically from the centre outwards, as though spilling out, or perhaps like Catherine Wheels spinning clockwise. At least they should be, but things can go wrong. Take the simple analogy of a bicycle wheel. Given a tap, if the wheels are well oiled, they will rotate on and on. But if the wheels are rusty so that some parts cannot move at all, effort must be made to rotate them.

When a chakra is 'dirty', it accumulates particles, like certain modern fabrics which seem to draw dirt to them after only one wash and never look clean. When the energy of a particular chakra remains unused, we cannot repel these particles, which are accumulating within the energy itself, and this causes malfunction. The energies cannot rotate as they should.

Alternatively, the energies may be whizzing around so furiously that the chakra becomes permanently over-charged and equally out of balance. In this case we must learn to switch them off, to de-activate them until we need the energy. The well-being of our physical body depends on the correct reception and distribution of energies and when the chakras are all evenly balanced, correctly awakened and energized, the body is in perfect harmony with the mind, emotions and spirit.

But most of us are far from perfect. Our chakras are in various stages of inertia or activity, and it probably shows. Someone may have stomach trouble, for example, and the effect of anything that upsets him will orientate towards that area. Obviously there is something causing him to react to life in that place and that place needs strengthening.

Each chakra reflects a quality, the quality of the colours that lie within it. And if, in simplistic terms, you are say, interested in physical sports, have a good sex life and enjoy learning, but are insensitive to psychic possibilities, you are probably working out of the lower chakras, oriented in the stomach and extremely earthed. If, conversely, you have psychic experiences such as premonitions or telepathy, are nervous and sensitive and disinclined towards physical life, then you are probably based in the top chakras and may equally be out of balance.

This book may be considered as an instruction manual on where we are on the scale of the psyche. It may be used to discover why we are the person we are, why we are oriented in this particular direction and why we are not fulfilling the potential within us.

We live on this earth. We are human beings. And as such we must live in harmony with our body. It is our main vehicle on earth. Our physical body is reflected in the etheric body and consequently in our chakras. Each chakra has a cord, attached to the spine, responsible for sending etheric circulation through the body. It is the chakras that receive energy from the Sun in the form of light. When light hits anything on the Earth it reflects back colour, or rather, as explained in the introduction it reflects back those colours which it does not absorb. So too when light hits our etheric body it reflects back the rainbow spectrum of colours and these are the colours in our chakras. Colour is energy.

It is the quality of these colours that reflects or state of being. The warm energies, the energies that fire our whole being, come from the base of our body. These are energies that move us to do things, the activating energies, and therefore, logically, the colour of the sexual energy, the source of human power, must be warm. The natural colour of the sex chakra is RED, and within that colour the state of the reproductive area is revealed; its health, and its history and its changes.

The digestive energy is again a warm colour, for this area too has a great deal of work to do. This is the ORANGE centre, which may indicate malfunction of the adrenals, for example, or ulcers, or disharmony in the gastric juices. If these two fundamental areas are inactive, then the top of the body is left waiting for the energies to rise, for energy to be brought up for use. The assimilation and digestion of food is a sacred process and in many people this area is unbalanced.

The YELLOW centre of the solar plexus chakra reflects, strangely, our state of mind and projects how we look at life intellectually. In physiological terms if reflects the left or rational side of our brain and the frustrations of the intellectual mind. Medically it indicates disharmonies in the organs such as the pancreas and liver, below the diaphram. Schizophrenics have a very bright overcharged solar disc. In ancient times seers deliberately overcharged this area by special breathing, taking a hallucinatory mushroom or other concoction. But to do this in safety they had to live a life of strict discipline and meditation.

GREEN is the natural colour of the heart centre – although the all-powerful mind can overule. The heart colour reveals how we relate to people and to nature. In other words, it indicates how much heart we put into our activities, and reflects our emotional life. Physically it shows how well the heart itself and the organs around it are functioning. It is a vulnerable centre and any abuse – drugs, too much medicine, too much coffee, being over-emotional – can leave a mark on the heart. Those who smoke create rings over the etheric body in that area.

From the BLUE of the throat centre we see how a person expresses himself, how he uses words to reflect his whole being, everything he feels. Physically this chakra shows up vulnerabilities around the throat. It is important to realize that, if for example the thyroid is out of balance, the whole body will be affected. Many people today have an imbalance in this area. The whole shoulder area takes the brunt of our cares.

Although the main energies collect in these concentrated areas, at the same time the whole energy field around the body encompasses and reflects the energy from individual areas. If the heart area is depleted this will affect the circulation which obviously affects other areas. Nothing works in isolation.

INDIGO is the natural colour of the brow chakra, reflecting the right or intuitive, non-verbal side of the brain. It shows our healing abilities, by indicating how much energy that area can gather, and also our outlook on healing. It shows sensitivity on the one hand and disharmony through mental imbalance on the other.

The VIOLET crown chakra makes clear the quality of our appreciation of art, religion and beauty and, through these, our link with the Creator.

Most of us are out of balance. We do not make perfect rainbows but predominate usually in one particular colour. We overcharge one centre, giving it far more energy than the others, and that colour shines too brightly. Visually, since the centre is resolving too fast, it will affect the chakras above and below and seem to take over.

If we overcharge in one area we naturally deplete in others. Everyone has depleted energy in one centre or another. If at times your mind feels fuzzy and you find it difficult to concentrate, then probably the solar plexus energies are out of balance. The world is not an easy place in which to live, especially today with so much upheaval and change. A mind overactive with worry will affect the solar plexus centre and through its proximity to the stomach this are too will suffer. If you lack energy, it is often the digestive centre that is depleted. If you menstruate heavily and feel pain at ovulation, then the sexual energies are acting negatively.

The heart reacts to things that have particular significance to our own conditioning in life. What one person reacts to with their heart, another may not react to at all. But the heart itself filters, like a computer, each of our emotions, large or small, from morning until night. It responds quickly on a physical level to almost every situation that we personally concerned about. When it does, our adrenalin levels rise, and with constant stimulation to stress or 'danger' our adrenals must suffer.

Today we hold in our emotional problems. We tend to sit on our worries, especially men who are drilled not to show pain, and this in turn adversely affects the heart. The heart, switched on and off like a light bulb by constant stimulation, will reach confusion point and eventually the bulb will explode. We can begin to see how our state of mind and emotions will affect various, linking aspects of our physical body.

The throat centre is the centre most under attack by bacteria and

when the throat energy is depleted it is open to all kinds of threat –
colds, tonsilitis, laryngitis, any kind of throat problem. A depletion in
this area, through an imbalance of the thyroid gland, can also lead to
being overweight. As we have said, all energies needed for action rise
from the base of the body and the more we can move this energy up to
the throat centre, the more we can cope with infection.

Depletion of the forehead centre means we meet stress on a more
psychic level. This area registers the affect of the 'unseen' on the body.
Someone sensitive may lose energy not only to the person with whom
he is directly speaking, but also find his energy is 'borrowed' from the
person behind him. Changes in the weather or phases of the moon will
affect such a person. Changes in the earth's vibratory rates will also pull
at his energies. Occurences which many people will deny because they
do not care to think about the different contacts we make on 'invisible'
levels.

Finally, if the crown centre, the area that regulates the whole of our
body is out of balance, everything feels off-key.

The vibrations of an energy centre show up all the defects of the
particular area it covers; people with weak chakras are always under
par because their bodies are constantly fighting to survive. And where
two depleted centres meet, the large area of depletion between them
will represent a double place of weakness and a greater risk of illness.

The better our energies in any one chakra, the more closely knit are
the vibrations of neighbouring chakras and the more we are protected.
Our chakras are like planets in the milky way – the milky way being
the other smaller energy centres all over the body. When all are
shining brightly we feel fit and well, but if there is any obstruction –
like a lump or a germ – part of that energy will die and this will show in
a depleted chakra.

Other problems arise when the two sides of our body are out of
balance. Energies cannot flow in an easy way. If the right shoulder is
lower than the left, then the muscles must constantly adjust, and
adjustment means the burning of food uneconomically. Older people,
for example, often use most of their food energy simply for moving
from one place to another. Their muscles have adjusted into the
wrong spaces. Someone with all his muscles in the correct place – a
virtual impossibility – is likely to eat less, since less energy is needed to
move the body; it just flows.

We will know, either through instinct or illness, when too much
energy is leaving the body: when colours are lacking and the chakras
are depleted. One of the most important things we need to keep our
bodies healthy is exercise. The chakras are pulled into activity by

movement. Our bodies are always fighting disease, but when the energies are made strong by exercise, the body can begin to know the difference, the joy of not fighting. Here is the value of yoga.

A yoga exercise formulated for one particular centre (see Chapter Five) will energize the whole surrounding area, and in any yoga movement there is something to move some section of our body. Often the exercise that is good for us is the one that hurts us most, the one that makes us miserable and uncomfortable. This is the one which produces the deepest movement within. These areas, stiffened through inactivity, are most full of toxins. The effort in making these centres move is often exhausting and not simply because the body is unsupple. Release of toxins might make the body ache, and when energies are half-dead, the exercise is tiring. Things previously cushioned by inactivity will come to the foreground and will often be painful. But once inactive areas are reactivated, the defence systems become stronger, we begin to look differently at our problems.

Each one of us is different. Each of us is composed of differently vibrating energies. Some of us have reached a stage in our development at which we are feeling our way into new fields of understanding. By trying to improve our knowledge, for example, or our intuitive powers, by increasing our potential, we are allowing a wider variety of vibratory rates into our system. We are constantly bombarded with differing vibratory rates from the cosmos and our ability to utilize them depends on our degree of evolution. And sickness will manifest from a variety of different causes even though symptoms may seem vaguely the same. This is why such disciplines as yoga are important. Unlike allopathic drugs, which treat symptoms only, yoga allows the body to heal itself by energizing the depleted areas.

Once the correct colour charge can enter a centre, if other colours infiltrate into the centre now and again – as they should according to our changing moods and needs – this will only be temporary. It is only when a wrong colour arrives in a chakra and remains there too long that life is changed in a negative way.

Part of the experience of keeping the body healthy comes through energies outside us. And part from the energies within, like the energy we create from food. It is the outer and the inner blending together that forms the right chemistry to produce health.

The body thrives on a set of vibratory rates. It must have vibratory food for harmony in the body.

Colour is vibration* and the seven colours of the spectrum, as explained in the introduction, vibrate at different rates. Colour exerts a powerful influence on the mind and emotions as well as the body. It is a vital force that deeply influences our lives.

To remain healthy we must be aware of the quality and diversity of colour in all our chakras. We each have a different colour range infinitely rich in colour combinations which cannot possibly be included here, but we do tend to predominate in one colour at any one time. When one centre shines bigger and brighter than the rest we tend to take on the characteristics of that colour. Of course the quality of that colour can vary. The more luminous and translucent the colours appear to be, the more sophisticated that person will be – the more 'aware'.

RED means love. It means courage and passion, and we can literally see red if we are attacked. Red means a quick fiery temper that soon dies away to nothing. Red is extremes of despair and elation. Red people put all their energy into the things that interest them; they are outgoing and giving. They find it easy to show their love for others. Red people enjoy the good things in life, and perhaps, since the emotions are less controlled, they are prone to overweight.

A coarser shade of red reveals a tyrant or despot. A man who will do anything to get what he wants. In its most dangerous aspect, red might mean a maniac; someone who loses control into madness.

Most of us have a period in our lives when we rebel, a time when the red centre shines brighter than the others. At puberty the sexual area becomes stronger once it is capable of reproduction. This is the time when children may become destructive, but provided they are offered more than discos and sex to occupy this excess of energy, these energies will subtly begin to change until other colours come into the chakra or the red itself becomes more ethereal. Incidentally, a person showing a more luminous red will never think twice about saving you from danger. It is interesting that some boxers do stay on the coarser red.

Put to good use, the underlying aggression of red can be beneficial. Red people make good soldiers. Smugglers and adventurers can be red. Those on the red ray like brighter colours and flamboyant clothes. A man on the basic etheric red will enjoy nude paintings and women with large breasts, which will take him back to the security of the womb experience. He will probably enjoy nude magazines and

* *Nuclear Evolution* by Christopher Hills, published by Centre Community Publications, goes into the nature of light and colour more fully.

passionate films. He will prefer rhythmic music, and dancing that moves the hips. He is aware of his physique and likes to make an impression with his body. He may be drawn to yoga to improve his body, perhaps to lose weight, but certainly not for its intellectual or spiritual aspects. He will notice other bodies and be concerned about his own virility, although exercise may be difficult for him because this does need concentration. He also needs to relax.

ORANGE people love any sporting activity that moves them to the point of exhaustion. For them a good training session ends when they can hardly walk. Orange people are always in a rush to get things done and unless they rush they are unhappy. They enjoy food very much and have quite large appetites – they may have food fads – but they manage to stay slim because they are always on the move.

An orange person is a good organizer – trade unionists are often on this ray. On the finer levels of the colour, if he doesn't put his hungry energy into sport, an orange person will want to help others enjoy themselves in all kinds of activity. It is the colour of action and protection and people who project orange are often protective of others.

Orange people are sociable; they like parties and people around them. They enjoy music with a beat – military music perhaps. They make good army men. They may prefer still-life pictures, of food and utensils; they are drawn towards sporty, loose-fitting and comfortable clothes.

Obviously orange people are fitter than red people because of the energy in the digestive centre, but an excess of orange means that the body never rests completely. Rest to an orange person is not a quiet, passive state of mind, but something that happens when he has tired himself out.

A YELLOW person probably goes to university and enjoys a life of study, but even if this is not the case he knows his worth and gets value for money. Scientists, politicians and business men are often yellow. A yellow woman may decide against marriage or if she does marry may put her career before her family. Someone yellow has a practical approach to life. He is seldom poor because he has the knack of making money and using it sensibly. Yellow is the colour of the sun and yellow people are stimulating.

Yellow people tend to ignore the body. They enjoy food but possibly not if they have to cook it constantly. They like clean-cut geometrical styles in clothes, often in brighter colours. They like to look good. Yellow people prefer more sophisticated and classical music but a wide variety of painting.

People who radiate on the lower chakras are busy, outgoing people, but as we move up the colour spectrum we meet people who are beginning to be aware of inner silence.

GREEN people are full of outflowing love and in return they will receive love from others. All love affairs bring overcharging on the green, but in a beautiful way. Nature loves a lover because She is always willing us to procreate. She gives us this radiance called love. Green people are aware of nature and have an affinity with plants. They make good gardeners and farmers.

Green, the combination of blue and yellow, means that the mind functions well but also indicates a good listener. Others will come to such people with their troubles. Green people enjoy children – nursery teachers are often green – and animals. A green person hates pollution and because he ranges into the blue ray he is drawn to water, lakes and sea. He is temperamentally more balanced than other colours and less easily offended because he makes excuses for people. On the other hand his soft heart means he is easily hurt. Green people are sentimental, they enjoy romantic music and paintings of landscapes and sky. They like clothes in subtle shades.

The more luminous the green, the more they will work for other people. But green people are never quite satisfied with themselves. They need to understand what is going on around them, to be aware of relationships and how they work. Often they have had some kind of emotional trauma or unhappiness. They know deep down that they should be the balancers in the spectrum and give tranquility to others. If they are out of balance themselves, they feel inadequate for the job.

PALE BLUE people have a quiet sense of aloofness; they do not rush up and hug you. They have a consciousness of inner silence and look out on the world with a sense of awareness that makes them observers. They notice other people's gifts. They notice the small things, and are not haphazard. The precision of pale blue makes a good engineer.

They may be untidy but do prefer an organized life around them. Politicians are often pale blue, and sailors, too, with a love of water. They like pictures of sky and sea; they appreciate Church music and chants, as well as classical. They like inconspicuous clothes that look right. They like to look clean and tidy. When they take up something, they hold on to it seriously in order to help others.

Pale blue people will be drawn to yoga because deep down they sense a path. They may attend a class for health or movement and not fully realize that a 'coincidence' has taken them there. Priests and clergy are often pale blue.

INDIGO people have a natural inclination towards the healing

services. They have a need to help people back to health on a deeper
level than the pale blue person. Doctors are often indigo. These people
have a stillness inside them and the greater that stillness, the more
ethereal the quality of the colour, the more it reflects. An indigo person
may not speak very much but we are made aware of ourselves through
him. He has a quality of mirroring back what we are.

They are composed, quiet people with a natural ability to make us
feel good. Often big and gentle, they can instill calm and well-being.
Priests have this colour and sometimes social workers who look after
the very sick or are drawn to prisons or mental institutions.

Indigo people make good yoga instructors, but they may prefer to
use their energies for healing. Healing should be performed through
incoming cosmic energies, and the more ethereal the colour, the
greater the ability to receive that cosmic energy and the greater the
healing power through use of the psychic part of the brain.

Indigo people like to wear blue. They like Church-like music and
paintings that are deeper and richer in colour; perhaps mystical
paintings and symbols. They like dark blue skies. They will work in
alternative medicine such as acupuncture and also psychology. They
will be drawn to yoga because they sense a block in themselves – that
energy is not flowing freely in some area of the body.

VIOLET people need admiration and love. They are sensitive, with
a need to express that sensitivity in many different fields. This may go
into art or music or even into a sense of fashion. It is the quality of the
artist, the painter.

Unless we have some violet within us we cannot appreciate beautiful
things – the only way to sense God in our world is through beauty.
Violet people are sensitive to lovely things. They like to be different
and to look different. Often they follow a bohemian lifestyle. They
tend to be disorganized. Fashion designers may have violet. Violet
people like unique and unusual paintings or, with a more ethereal
quality, spiritual and religious paintings.

Violet is a mix of blue and red and if the red is more prominent then
this could take a more sexual form of expression. A blue bias is a
different realm altogether. On the spiritual side are people with visions,
and as with all artists there will be a need to go inside themselves at
times. A need to be constantly creating. Sculptors are violet.

If yellow creeps into the blue and red mix of violet, we have an
allied colour MAGENTA. In addition to the violet qualities we see
someone who can administrate. Someone who has a love of beauty but
also the gift to organize it.

The way we see things around us will be influenced by one

predominant chakra. Someone working out of the heart chakra will see a child as an object of love. Someone on the red ray will remember the sex act which created him. A spiritually-oriented person will think of his soul and a mind-oriented person will be concerned with his intellect.

We are all colour biased.

Although this book is concentrating on the main energy centres of the body, we do have chakras all over the body. The whole of our body has a circulation of energy patterns which flow right through the body from head to toe. The acupuncture points are minute energy centres which produce a wider picture of the state of our being. Like the stars in the milky way, the whole body is radiating light.

As we eliminate the vibrations we do not need, there is a constant release of energy from the body. It may happen in bursts or in one steady stream, but the sum total of this release of energy, or in other words, the etheric field around us, is called the *aura*. The aura is coloured by our feelings. When we sense unconsciously a need for a special colour we are drawn towards that vibration, perhaps by choosing clothes, food or another human being who is that colour. When a more advanced person needs a certain colour energy he can consciously produce this in the aura.

People who overcharge in one particular chakra will tend to produce that colour in the aura too. However, the overall colour of the aura tends to change with our moods, the place we are in and the people we are with. When someone else comes close to us there is an interchange, like an electrical storm, which sparks as the two auras blend.

Whatever we are, the aura will manifest it in some way and everything around us will affect it, but in fact it is the *feel* of the aura rather than the colour that is important. We ourselves form the fabric of our aura. When we are strong the aura is resilient; when we are fixed it becomes harder. And since the aura is made up of vibratory rates released from the body, they differ from different parts of the body; some are stronger, some lighter.

The aura is made out of attractions. We attract what we deserve. When we radiate, we attract vibrations from the world around us; from plants, from the universe. We can always sense an attractive, glowing person. He seems to attract attention no matter where he sits, no matter where he goes. His aura will attract the attention of the cosmos and everything around it.

In this way the aura is also a protection. When we attract all the right things we are protected. The Church talks of Grace and you can tell from the aura, not just health patterns but also the kind of relationship a person has with the cosmos. A 'spiritual' person glows in the dark. If he walks into a room he is quickly noticed.

Snails have feelers at the top of their heads, but our system is far more complicated. We have feelers all round our bodies – Kirlian photography has proved we have tiny feelers beyond our fingers and we can 'touch' another person's aura. Where those feelers stretch out at the end of the aura there is usually a rainbow effect, where the sun meets the force of energy released from the body. As the light splits up it forms a rainbow and as the shafts of light penetrate through to our own energy fields they are drawn into the centres according to their colour range.

Or should be. It is not quite as simple as that. It is our feeling of what we are that constantly draws things to us. And if, for example, we negate the green, the love energy, from its rightful place in the heart centre, the green ray will have to find a home wherever it can. By negating colours we can cause disruption in the energy fields around us, especially if they go into areas in which they do positive harm. Thus we have the power to destroy ourselves or the power to create ourselves. We are in charge and it is up to us to allow in the right colours. Our business is to have more light to radiate beautifully.

The aura has a scent, just as the body does, and it changes. We smell sweet when we feel full of life and the aura sparkles like a cosmic display of fireworks. When the aura is dull and dingy we have 'aura odour'.

We are surrounded by and are flowing and floating in ether – like fish in water. If we swim well we survive better. Provided we use the flow of this substance we can rejuvenate our bodies. Ether is pliable and each time we think, it forms into a shape. These 'thought forms' float around us and crowd the invisible world – which is why it is sometimes uncomfortable to be with someone whose mind is churning. The etheric quality of a room can be changed by different forms and shapes. The movement inside can collect, transmute and change the colour of the ether. If you enter a room where two people have quarrelled the perfume hangs in the ether and remains even after they have left.

Negative thoughts, then, are shapes. These shapes flow into the aura and interrupt positive vibrations from the cosmos. Negative thoughts attract negative vibrations – from the earth and from others around us – and in the end the aura becomes a storehouse for negativity. This is why some people have brittle, broken and unhealthy auras – which also shows up in Kirlian photography. Eventually the physical body is deeply affected. We can see how the body and the world react upon each other.

Objects also change the ether in a room. Books, magazines, pictures, furniture vibrate and all contribute to the etheric quality in a room. If we worry we leave these vibrations to hover in the house. It is better to find a special corner where you can worry for an hour and fill the rest of the house with peace. A grimy corner is easier to clean than the whole house!

The shape of the aura is created by the volume and pressure of energies cascading up around us and down to be absorbed into the earth. We have energies below our feet and those of the feet themselves are important. If our feet stop radiating this probably means a stroke and it is interesting to note that the feet radiations of epileptics usually malfunction before an attack. The monitoring of feet radiations could be a useful source of preventive medicine.

Highly evolved people often have emanations of energy over the top of the head, so we can see the need for balance. When energies on the right side of the body do not measure equally the ones on the left (which often happens because people develop one side of their body more than the other); when the energies from the feet do not coordinate with the energies over the head, or when one foot radiates more than another, we are losing our basic egg shape in which we should be cocooned in the aura. We lose our shape.

The aura is always changing, but there does come a time when, within that change, we can reach a platform from which we view change in a different way. The more a person advances, the more in tune he is with himself, the more giving and loving, the less vulnerable is his aura to change. When it becomes sufficiently strong to allow finer qualities, it does not change. And, then, when you walk into a room, it is the room that changes, not you.*

There are people who can fill a room with their auras, and those whose auras will shrink or go grey. Some people do not change their own auras a great deal but change those of other people. And this can happen in two ways, one positive, one negative. When two personalities come together, the dominant may influence the weaker. In other words he will impose his colour on the other and often when we are depressed in a partnership we are experiencing this kind of

---

* A woman's aura changes during ovulation, which explains why she is more attractive to men at this time.

negative domination. A more spiritual person will restore his partner's aura, not impose his own.

Today we all have the capacity to see much much more. If we allow ourselves to observe we can learn. One person may look at someone and say 'Hello, how are you?'. Another will say 'Come on, you're ill, do something.' The second person has taken a good look, which many of us do not do. We do not feel the texture of a room or sense the atmosphere. We do not look at anything deeply.

To see more we have to look at everything in depth, and this means really caring. When we learn to care something is set in motion. Whether it is a jewel or a fabric or a person, everything vibrates and we can resonate in relation to its beauty.

We do not ask questions any more. We grow out of them. At the age when a child asks questions he easily accepts colour as an all-pervading energy; he can understand it because it is part of his world. But this gift is either not explained to him or he is talked out of it. And as he grows older he stops asking questions.

Today we do not realize how colour affects us, how it changes our mood. Even blind people can feel and react to colour, so the barrier is within us. If we let ourselves think what colour is doing, we may begin to see how it relates to human beings. Look at a warm, glowing red. Who do you know who *is* warm and glowing? Look at a cool blue. Who do you know who is cool, calm, collected — and blue? People vibrate on different levels. At a theatre or a disco there is a different colour to each situation, and if we stop, look and love deeply, we will begin to see. Slowly our consciousness will evolve. More and more people are beginning to see what extraordinary and beautiful beings we are and that it is up to us to help ourselves become more truly aware.

CHAPTER TWO

Red: Fire in the Basement

The warm energies have the slowest wave lengths but the greatest stimulative power. And, surprisingly in the so-called promiscuous age, it is these areas that are most commonly inactive.

Trouble, it seems, begins in the basement and more often than not it is the sexual area that is out of balance, through underuse, misuse, or overuse. So what is sex? Why do we get sensations that at times go off by themselves out of our own control?

The sexual, like all other centres, is simply a certain kind of energy. Any energy can be pumped and it is when the energies are pumped that they grow. Obviously this is what we are doing during intercourse. The chakra wheels spin in constant motion but during intercourse we are stepping up vibrations in the lowest centre. This is the most natural and profitable way of sufficiently pumping up the energies for use by the higher centres. Once the vibrations reach a certain volume, they set off up the body, touching the next chakra and this begins to spin too.

Like wheels in motion, one wheel sets the next one moving. And this is why during intercourse feelings begin in the basement and seem to rise. Quite often we feel sensation rising to the heart and it is when it reaches the throat that we call out or make throat sounds. Climactic sensations vary, but if the energies reach the top of the head we may go dizzy. The energy can actually go beyond the crown until we feel lifted out of this world.

This is the reason, should we wish to explain it, why some people enjoy being hurt for pleasure. These energies are whipped more and more, which is not the same as pumping. If a child pumps his humming top it will spin, but if he whips away the string it goes crazily into a very fast spin. If basement energies are whipped they explode through all the chakras, shooting the sensations up and beyond into ecstasy. But what is not fully understood is, firstly, that this can ruin the chakras, and, secondly, that sexual activity is more fulfilling if the chakras are 'opening' naturally.

When chakras begin to open, sexuality is experienced on a more spiritual level and once the basement chakra is open, for example, the energies when pumped no longer whirl in the same way. With cosmic energies coming in from the outside we experience a deeper merging, with high vibrational energy above the head. As this comes down more energies rise up through the body, which can take in yet more energy from the cosmos. A rare and beautiful climactic experience produces a more spiritual than physical sensation.

The prevailing colour of the chakra shows our *current* experience, whether we are using our energies properly or not. The reproductive energies of someone who has no sex or exercise at all will show up as brown and opaque. Too much sex (depending on each individual) will turn them metallic. (It depends on your state of health how quickly they become metallic and having sex when you are tired or working too hard may prove just as harmful as too much sex.) If we have black in any chakra, which indicates an emotional or health imbalance, the energy cannot reach the momentum it needs to rise to the top of the head. It becomes stuck and a climax is not achieved.

Today we sit around; in the car, watching television, in the office. And consequently there are many inactive basements. Walking, standing and sitting can drain the sexual energies simply through lack of exercise. And, without exercise, this can become progressively worse as we grow older. Operations on the prostate gland, for example, are now necessary far earlier; the average age today is just over forty. One of the simplest yoga exercises for the prostate is to sit on the floor and bring the head to the knee, but most men cannot do this.

The purpose of life is to evolve consciousness until it becomes one with the light that creates it. 'In the beginning was the Light.' And since the rainbow is the product of white light our purpose is to become a perfect rainbow. In the meantime, our centres are full of vibrations in the form of colours that often should not be there. These indicate the prevailing climate of our being. They are momentary and can be changed.

RED should be in the reproductive area and rarely in any other, and when red does appear in other centres there is always some kind of imbalance. Out of context, red will be associated with

AGGRESSION and IRRITATION.*

If RED forms in the ORANGE digestive centre, energy accumulates there instead of going freely up the spine as it should. This will produce some kind of stomach trouble. It can happen either when, through misuse of the sexual area, the red area is overcharged and runs into orange, or when the area is underused. Without a boost from the sexual energy, the stomach has to supply sufficient energy for both the sexual area and its own. Without help from below it needs to be noticed and the less sex we have the more we are oriented in the stomach, the more our interest in food to provide instant energy — probably sweet things.

Incidentally, it is difficult to maintain the red energy at the right level. Without sufficient sex, a build-up of that energy can cause problems. A sporty person may use the energy for running, others for mind activity or helping people. But those who cannot activate the centre in any other way may revert to the imagination. They will boost the energy by eyeing pretty girls or perhaps through pornography.

It is possible to raise the sex energy for studying. But often RED in the YELLOW mind centre means that a person is using the energy for sex in the imagination. Taking the mind on sexual trips will eventually irritate that centre and adversely affect the mind. The red of irritation appears in the mind chakra when things are going badly, when relationships have broken down and fate seems to be against us. When red reaches the brain we see red.

RED in the GREEN, heart centre, can mean two things. It may mean tremendous emotional love and it probably is not good to have love of such passion in this area. Or it may mean we have been deeply hurt. The red looks like blood oozing from the heart and brings a reality to the expression 'my heart bleeds for him'.

RED in the PALE BLUE, throat centre, is the bane of public speakers. It usually means swollen glands and irritation.

RED in the INDIGO, forehead centre, is connected with the psychic. Of course there are many shades of red and a deep carnation pink, for example, would mean a strong love for humanity, but deep red will only bring gross sensitivity. Passion and emotion take over and there is complete inability to control the psyche. Often it is the sign of someone who is mentally sick. It is interesting to note that drug takers and schizophrenics have red in most of their centres.

* The colours in the crown centre are an indication of something entirely separate and different and will be dealt with in a later chapter.

Orange: Move Into Action

The digestive energy is, if anything, more important than the sex energy. It keeps us alive. But as we become more sensitive to life and each area is saturated by other colours, the stomach, too, is no longer the place – in a sensitive person – where only the digestion of food takes place.

To take all sensitivity from that area would probably be wrong, but the stronger we can make that area and the more control we have over the muscles, the less we need fear the other colours that flow there. When the digestive centre is strong, the other colours that come in may even be useful.

The point of yoga is to pump the energies up towards the top of the body. It is the warm base energies, which change to a high vibration as they move upwards, that fuel the body. And it is these that eventually help to open the dormant parts of our brain.

We use most meals as a focal point for social activity and everything else that passes through our minds and bodies, and colours our centres, will, according to the amount of sensitivity in the body at the time, have an affect on the stomach area. Eating, then, although a pleasant experience, can be hazardous for someone sensitive.

Apart from allowing other colours into the area, we may use the digestive centre for cognition. It is the area in which we register something that is about to happen – our psychic receptor. We may feel butterflies or a sinking in the stomach before a major event or before we meet someone.

The ancients looked closely at the digestive centre. Purity and cleanliness were essential to any kind of progress, and when this area was not functioning properly it impaired the yellow centre above it. They thought a dirty intestine would affect the mind itself. It is therefore an important part of yoga to bring back the strength and quality of the digestive area. By bringing in a more spiritual shade we can register the more spiritual aspect of our nature. In this area we are feeding the whole of our being, and we cannot bring about any permanent and meaningful changes unless we realize this.

Sensitivity in the stomach can bring fear and tension, which may lead to ulcers. The stomach is often our first reactor to infection and if it is under bacterial attack or feels we are polluting it, it will quickly let go of everything! It has a resourceful mind of its own, but it will also compensate far longer than any other centre. It will function with very little goodness until it reaches a point of no return. Then it will simply refuse to function.

Our aim is to make it possible not only for us to harden the stomach for use as the base of our strength, but also for us to take any emotional blows in the stomach itself. If a car stops within an inch of us, most of us react with a thumping heart. But we should be able to react by contracting our stomach muscles. When these relax a few seconds later the heart and pulse are normal, and he can walk away calmly. By doing so he can relieve the heart from some of its pressures. No matter how much heart we put into something, unless we have a corresponding amount of energy we cannot achieve very much.

The depletion of one area automatically affects the area next to it. A depletion of the reproductive area stops proper digestion and if, for example, there is over-stimulation of the energy above it, then the digestive centre is caught between them, not knowing whether it is coming or going.

Once we have a stomach area healthy and unaffected by emotion, it shines a bright vivid orange. Vegetarians, incidentally, show a more gentle shade of orange and this should be watched. A softer shade might mean anaemia, and Yogis often wore orange robes to compensate for the lack of meat.

ORANGE is not simply the colour of digestion: it symbolizes active energy. Shine an orange beam on to an object and it seems to come to life. So when ORANGE is drawn into the other chakras, the operative word is ACTIVITY.

In fact ORANGE seldom does appear in other chakras, except perhaps into the RED, reproductive area, which suggests a more sporty sex life. In this case sex is a friendly, outgoing arrangement, a healthy way to release tension. But with ORANGE only in this centre there will be little depth to the sex life. It will be fulfilling in the same way that other sport is fulfilling.

ORANGE seldom appears in the YELLOW mind centre, but if it does it suggests an athletic mind. Someone with stomach energies in the mind centre will have a frisky brain. He will like mental puzzles such as crosswords, jigsaws or chess. Some people sleep on trains, he will use his mind for some active fun.

ORANGE, too, is seen rarely in the GREEN, heart chakra. The heart is not normally associated with exercise – unless for body-building, in which case you must be careful not to put red into the heart as well. To use up the ORANGE energy and then fall back on the reproductive energy – which you can do by exercising a great deal – the pumping of these energies around the heart area will bring on a climactic experience. If this experience is pursued, the RED will stay in that centre after a time and may cause a heart attack.

Nor is ORANGE seen often in the PALE BLUE, throat centre. It

could only be drawn there by people who use that area for both
activity and the voice. Umpires and referees, perhaps, who use their
voices and run at the same time. Or a trained soldier, who screams his
orders as he runs with his men.

ORANGE is seldom in the INDIGO, forehead centre. Except
perhaps in someone who is motivated towards spirituality through
hard work rather than meditation. Someone who does not care for a
lonely meditative life, but prefers to actively use the stomach energies
in doing mundane tasks for others.

Yellow: A Mind of Our Own

Primitive man was aware of elemental life. He had mystical
experiences. He saw nature spirits and angels. The yellow aspect, the
intellect, was not yet developed so he could not control the things he
saw with his mind. He protected himself with ritual signs and amulets,
not logic. People were affected by curses through the intuitive side of
their nature. With the light of logic man cannot be destroyed. Curses
worked because there was too little logic and constructive thought to
analyse what made these curses so powerful.

The primitive sent their hearts out to nature with love and awareness
and could be in tune with their surroundings. But it made them
vulnerable. The stomach area, too, was vulnerable, because psychic
awareness is registered here. The ancients, the Aztecs and Atlanteans,
realised the potential in energizing the Sun disc (the area around the
solar plexus) because of its connection with the mind. The Sun was the
centre of the universe. Once the yellow centre is developed (particularly
if it shows the gold of wisdom) the radiations will annihilate the
negativity in the other side of the brain.

So an area grew between the GREEN and ORANGE centres
which could control the two and prevent them swinging negatively too
fast or too slow. This central wheel was vital in order for the other two
to function properly. By learning more about them they could be
maintained in harmony.

Man produced this yellow energy to study the emotions both
within the digestive area and the heart. The mind, emotions and food
are closely linked, and by uniting the centres insight could grow.
There was no need for ritual because psychic warfare could be cut off
with logic. The left and right sides of the brain could combine.

Sadly, the balance has swung right across and rationality has become
all powerful. We now dissect everything and this area predominates as
education becomes more complex. In some people it has displaced all
the other colours and made it difficult for them to sense any kind of

spirituality. They have become too ego conscious and cut off from the other aspects of their being.

YELLOW in the yellow centre is fine in someone who needs impartiality. It is a good receiving station, good for study and the retention of facts. But ideally he needs a glowing heart centre, too, to balance him out. Once the yellow centre stands out beyond all others you find an eccentric who thinks only of himself, motivated into making himself a brilliant academic and successful in any field.

The yellow centre is dependent upon all the others, and if these are misused the yellow will crack and affect the brain itself. Drugs, for example, may stimulate the brain for a while, but eventually they will blacken the other centres and finally destroy the yellow one too.

When yellow appears in chakras other than the yellow, we are taking the mind into all our other energies. Yellow is ANALYTICAL. About everything. A little yellow in any centre is useful because some logic in all areas of our lives is necessary.

With YELLOW in the RED centre, a person's attitude to sex is governed by the mind. If he is not with the one he loves, he will love the one he is with. Often, because of something that has happened in his life, he has brought his emotions under such control that he is incapable of love. He has little warmth. Consequently he may need a wide variety of sexual activity because this is the only way to fulfill himself. The mind as well as the body becomes bored and needs new kicks. But nothing is lasting.

YELLOW in the ORANGE digestive centre means the stomach is so well controlled that few emotions are registered there. But psychic sensitivity is also cut off. People like this have no time for sickness, so stomach trouble will annoy them because their mind cannot deal with it. People, they feel, should get on with their lives, not sit around moaning and they will even be unsympathetic to a sick child. He, too, should put up with things. Women with yellow in orange will often choose not to have children because they are too self-oriented. And even when they do have children they will probably put themselves or their work first.

YELLOW in the GREEN heart centre, is a sign that a person is trying to control the emotions in his heart with his intellect. If he has gone through the hopeless pain of rejection, he will now be too frightened to give his heart deeply. He will like any partner he is with well enough, but he will be incapable of real love. But since the mind enjoys the diversity of different relationships he will need constant changes to play with the superficial elements of love. Yellow is associated with fear and yellow in the heart is the colour of the coward.

A coward who cannot allow his heart to be captured.

YELLOW in INDIGO, the forehead centre, is good in that it is better for healers to be slightly cool and analytical or they may become involved with their patients and live through their tragedies. Impartiality in healing is important and some yellow in the forehead means a balanced personality. A healer with yellow will not simply be using a strange gift he happens to have, but will know exactly what he is doing. In healing we need a deep understanding of the energies we are allowing to come through our own body and into another's.

YELLOW in the PALE BLUE, throat centre, means someone who is clever but who needs to prove it constantly. There is little kindness with yellow in the throat. It belongs to a person who likes to score points. A writer, for example, with this colour, will be an intellectual trying to express something, but at the same time trying to prove things about the natural world. He will want his work to be scientific but if it is not he will make things *sound* so clever that they are given a larger reality. When he does not understand something he will find a clever way of relating to it, which cannot in fact be very deep.

Green: The Heart of the Matter

Life was first realized through the instinctive side of our being. In primitive times it was deeply concerned with eating and reproduction, when the lower aspects of our being were prominent. Like the dinosaurs, which had small heads and huge bodies, our energies were oriented at the base of the body. This must occur when energy is needed to survive. A wild cat, if it is reared domestically and knows where its meals are coming from, has the opportunity to enlarge and balance its higher chakras and is far less likely to attack than a predatory cat in the wild whose energy is used to find food. Some of the instinctive aggression will diminish.

When our needs were oriented more towards the stomach, our sexual area was also boosted because one affects the other. The more domesticated man became, with the introduction of agriculture, the more he know where he would eat next, and the less obsessed he became with the stomach area. Consequently, the sexual instinct became more refined too. In the ancient days because these two centres were brightest, it was often thought that the two colours were one, since they governed the basic needs.

The heart is the seat of the soul. It is the heart that makes us human. Love is the guiding principle of life. But until this moment in evolution, we have been unable to manifest this higher level. Emotion was registered in the stomach and even now if we are hurt and cannot love fully with the heart we go back to our more primitive selves and sense things through the stomach. Psychic ability often opens during times of great stress and emotional turmoil.

As we began to acquire our logical understanding and produce the yellow ray within us, we began to appease the gods with logic, where before we had appeased them with love and care and work. Naturally we had to go through various stages of cleansing and purification before we reached the right kind of yellow, but logic has now become all-powerful and we need to bring back the purer qualities of the heart.

Mankind is now moving into the heart centre in which the soul can manifest. It is a danger period for the Earth because as we swing into the whole of Nature, we can either move smoothly into this area of energy with understanding or we can cause tremendous turmoil. We are affecting nature not only through pollution but also through the green chakra of our emotions.

In order to have a secure and beautiful world we must concern ourselves deeply with the Earth. We must take the responsibility to heal Nature around us. Only then will she heal us. We must realize more than ever that she is our healing and our nourishment, and in some way we must communicate with the very soul of Nature, which keeps us alive and which is linked not only to the elementals but also to the higher forces. A group soul that is living and breathing on the green centre, in the same way as we are living on our own green centre.

Most of us have covered this area with vibratory rates or colours that provide us with a safety valve. Fear produces other colours in our centres. And when we are hurt we protect ourselves. The only way to purify the heart is to lose our over-riding fear of being left alone. We must understand the myth about security. Only then can we have a true understanding of relationship.* Only then will the heart be ready to merge with a higher consciousness, ready to work for love in its true sense.

Of course there are varying shades but all too often there is very little green in the green area. The heart reacts to every emotion, and those who lack green are retreating from further pain. All of us have experienced bereavement or rejection by someone we love. A darker shade of green means possessiveness and jealousy; brown or black means the area is miserable and cannot express the part which is lovable. The centre is out of balance.

Some people do mend their own hearts. Nature is very healing and

* See Annie Wilson, *The Wise Virgin*, Turnstone Press (1979).

by being deeply in tune this can happen. It can lift out the pain and maintain the right colours. When Green appears in other centres the energy is SENSITIVE and ADAPTABLE.

GREEN in the RED, reproductive centre means that the heart goes into the sex life. We can never be promiscuous and if something goes wrong with the sexual relationship, we will need a special, gentle kind of loving and understanding. It is not the variety of activity that matters but the amount of love given at the moment of contact. A sexual relationship can only be one of deep love.

Sensitive people often put GREEN in the ORANGE digestive centre and their psychic stomach will beat almost like a heart. They are vulnerable not only to their own emotions but also to those of other people. They are affected by everything in life, even past memories. Things about to happen will register deeply in the stomach. People who have over-run the stomach with green should be careful in what they eat because this can lead to digestive problems. But if they can also pull some yellow into the area the two together will give greater balance.

If we have no GREEN at all in the YELLOW mind centre, we have a one-sided approach to life. We meet our goals with no consideration of the heart. If we do have our heart in this area it will show in how warm and generous we are; the shade of green will indicate how much we give with friends.

With no GREEN in the PALE BLUE throat centre, there is little warmth. With a little green a person is kind. But with too much green he is in danger of being used by other people. He lacks the strength to refuse people and they will walk over him. It may also indicate someone who heals through herbs.

Too much GREEN in the INDIGO forehead centre suggests that kidness is taking over. This for a healer is bad. He will rush to help people even though he may not be sufficiently qualified. Too little green suggests a person who does things for other people but not out of love. This is probably better for a healer who will not then become too involved with his patients.

Blue: Words of Wisdom

Primitive man had so many other senses developed that the throat, the organ of speech, was far less important. He made his communication on a different, silent, inner level, and noise was used for his more basic needs. Noise was associated with the red and orange centres, with sexual arousal or of being hungry or in danger. Noises were made when predators or prey were near.

Articulate speech and the colours of speech were something developed later. Primitive man 'knew' everything about the elements, but he could not control them. Now, using our logical mind, to some extent we control our environment. We work with nature in a different way. When we had learned this skill, we needed speech to articulate it, and this chakra is now pronounced. Once children could no longer learn by instinct, we needed speech to teach them.

Through evolution, the centre has become larger and as we have evolved from the lower centres, the coolness of the human being has come into play. But just as the ancient yogis knew they must undergo periods of silence to conquer any negativity of the speech centre, we too should now try to be more silent, more meditative, in order to tune once more into nature's higher needs.

Every area of life can be raised to a higher art form, and we have now made an art form of the throat area. Where prophets once worked from the red centre, we have lecturers who are eloquent, cool speakers.

Christ healed a great deal simply by talking, by using the vibration of sound. In the future sound will become an important method of healing. As the ancient civilization in Atlantis proved, the body can be brought into perfect harmony through sound. Music plays a vital part in this, although much of modern music actually does harm. Rock music can upset the harmony and balance of the body. But the voice, too, is important and illness can be affected by such sound. Think how much we can tell from a person's voice; we can begin to learn what vibrations we are using when we talk. When we are repetitive the colours in this area become fixed. If we are always moaning the colours are dull and will affect the thyroid. If we are silent we shall have white in that area.

Depending on how we feel and how we express ourselves the throat area will change, but in opening the psyche properly we must remember to take care of the area around the eyes, around the ears, the back of the neck and head. Unless we can move that area freely we will have repercussions as we open spiritually. Spiritual people tend to look younger because through greater awareness the muscles of the eyes, ears and in the back of the head are functioning well. The colours in the throat contribute to this and a beautiful smile makes the throat centre glow. Indeed, most centres react to smiling.

Blue in any other centre represents COOLNESS.

A small amount of PALE BLUE in the RED reproductive centre need not be harmful, but generally it indicates a cool slightly more calculated approach to sex. ICE BLUE means that disappointment or hurt in a relationship has caused coolness towards sexual relationships.

BLUE in the ORANGE digestive centre is not a healthy sign. Food is approached on a mundane, unimaginative level and, after all, we cannot survive if we do not eat.

Depending on the shade of BLUE in the YELLOW mind centre, this can indicate a cool, clear head in teaching and lecturing. The ability to give out knowledge without becoming emotionally involved. ICE BLUE means that the mind is becoming hard and cold.

BLUE in the GREEN heart centre is not so good. When ICE BLUE appears it is like ice over a pond. We cannot respond to love and avoid new relationships. Perhaps we are cooling ourselves down – putting ourselves on ice – to mend that area, but it makes us cool and aloof.

The paler the BLUE in the INDIGO, forehead centre, the more this represents healing through the voice rather than through the laying on of hands.

Indigo: Other Ways of Seeing

Situated in the forehead centre is the Third Eye. The eye of the psyche. It might be described as the dial of a radio with which we can tune in to any age we have been before. The forehead, then, is a tuning-in instrument, a visionary apparatus which is healthily sensitive can be used in a positive and controlled way. The Third Eye is sensitive of people's thoughts and feelings, but it also shows the different lives we have led in the past and, what is more, since it comes full circle, those we will lead in the future. The quality of our current life is affected by successive incarnations.

In the Third Eye, as in the ordinary eye, are tiny segments which represent life experiences – a television monitor with us in the middle. A personal record. The sum total of this and previous life experiences that makes us what we are today. Our files are alive and operational, and if as seers we can stand in the centre of our own or another's third eye, we can take out whichever file we want. To adjust our Third Eye is like adjusting to a wireless station. If we are more evolved in Third Eye awareness, we can tune in and adjust to that moment in time. It is a marvellous mechanism with so many different layers of consciousness that we can experience the whole of evolution; we can travel in and out of time and space.

The Third Eye is a complicated structure. Just as the iris of the ordinary eye will show up our physical illnesses (the therapy of iridology), the coarse etheric Third Eye (the densest level) shows our health patterns and mistakes from past lives, and how our body chemistry has changed with our growth. If, for example, we have a life in which we were stabbed through the heart, we will have deep emotional repercussions in that area during the next life. In the following life this will be diminished and instead we will probably have accumulated something else. Imagine a record with grooves. When something traumatic occurs in a life, it leaves a dent of discolouration.

The wrong or right vibrations going into the Third Eye will change our consciousness and something that went wrong hundreds of years ago may take until now to sort itself out. When we have too many colours in our Third Eye we may be attracted to many different past lives and attracted to various groups of people. It is better to keep to its natural deep blue or to white, but this rarely happens. Incidentally, when 'disoriented' people live with ten personalities simultaneously it seems they are becoming all the people in their past lives at the same time.

The top part of the Third Eye indicates our path towards achieving and in the base of the Third Eye are our deep pasts. We experience our Third Eye in spiral circles, each time dipping into our deep pasts, being touched by them but aware of the changes we have gone through since we last saw that deep aspect of our being.

The Third Eye can also be used, perhaps unconsciously, by actors who have been able to empty all colour out of their forehead, and then can pour in the colour they need at the time for a particular effect. If you want to change very quickly from laughter to tears, if you want to have black moods or green moods alternately, then you have to be able to beam in whatever colour you need. This can be dangerous because the colour will affect the whole body. Once you can tune into one particular colour so deeply that it replaces the other colours, you will find you can completely change your personality. Someone who is depressed and produces dark colours in the Third Eye will attract all kinds of negative qualities and everything will be full of melancholy and depression. We have therefore to be careful and learn control.

The Third Eye, then is an instrument of inner and outer awareness. In the finer etheric levels we get true cognition. But on top of this, as in any chakra, we register the colours we are working through in our present life. Colours in the Third Eye are specially significant and can tell us much. If we talk of the coarser etheric eye, inner aggression will manifest itself as an illness in the Third Eye in the red spectrum; greed will manifest in the orange, and envy in the green. All these produce symptoms in the Third Eye and are sensed by the body. They are then transformed into an organic state of illness. Christ said we should first cast out the beam in our own eye. We suggest he meant that if we heal the Third Eye first we have a greater chance of healing the whole body. Balancing the Third Eye is a collossal task and this we will deal with more fully later.

Indigo in centres other than the forehead indicates IMPARTIALITY.

INDIGO seldom occurs in the RED reproductive centre, but means that we are trying to use the sexual area for cognition of some kind.

INDIGO will only occur in the ORANGE digestive centre if the stomach is overcharged in some way.

INDIGO in the YELLOW mind centre indicates a cool, impartial man; a doctor who gives his patients 'extra' healing but is unaware he is doing so and is uninvolved in psychic matters.

INDIGO, the colour of healing with impartiality, seldom appears in the GREEN heart centre except in people who have a natural ability to heal with their hands, for nature or others. They are calm people because they have reached the stage at which their abilities flow naturally through them.

INDIGO rarely appears in the BLUE throat centre. It may indicate someone who heals with the voice, a hypnotist perhaps, or a mother who is singing a lullaby to her child.

Violet: We Are Our Past Lives

Violet is a colour we must all have since it is part of the spectrum. Where it radiates immediately from the top of the head centre, it signifies the artistic quality within our personality, our sense of the good and beautiful in life.

Violet in the other chakras, too, means a sense of ART and BEAUTY.

VIOLET in the RED reproductive centre indicates that sex must be artistic and beautiful. It cannot be brash or obscene.

VIOLET in the ORANGE digestive centre means that we like our food to look nice and to bless it before we eat. Some people with cosmic energy flowing in might even substitute food with suitable breathing exercises.

VIOLET in the YELLOW mind centre means we appreciate beauty but more logically. An artist who looks for symmetry and enjoys the way colours are put together, who knows why he likes or dislikes something.

VIOLET in the GREEN heart centre, shows a need for a spiritual relationship. The heart appreciates a beauty which analysing would destroy.

VIOLET in the BLUE throat centre shows an ability to express things verbally in an artistic way. Both yellow and violet in this area suggests a good art critic. Expression of the appreciation of art with knowledge.

VIOLET in the INDIGO forehead centre shows healing through the arts; using dance and music and drawing as therapy.

But there are colours that radiate further beyond this first etheric level and these have a far wider significance. Here we go beyond body consciousness. The colours that radiate from the crown register our whole state of being. They are not colours that change with the moment, that flow in and out. They are influenced to some extent by the colours in the other centres, but also by other kinds of interference, both visible and invisible. They register our soul experience, our state of consciousness. They are often qualities we have taken from different past lives. The soul evolving dedicates different lives to producing certain colours. It adds those colours and keeps them. The ancients described them as the 'many-petalled lotus'. They can also be described as a huge diamond with many sides. The formation of this diamond comes through the criss-crossing of energies and where they cross they flash like mirrors. If someone's diamond is clean and polished, we can see ourselves as other people see us. They reflect us back as we really are. The shinier the diamond, the higher the consciousness.

The diamond itself has three different aspects. The first is a crystalline layer which holds within it the progress we have made on the etheric level, a record of the state of our chakras, everything we are concerned with in this present life.

The second layer is more advanced and registers higher vibrations, when the mind takes over the emotions and we begin to see life not in fragments but as an overall creation. With this new awareness the basic chakras are changed and this indicates that many of the stumbling blocks on the personality level have been worked through. Only those that need working out on a higher level remain.

Even higher is another layer, which creates the total effect of a triple crown. The colours here are the final requisites of the soul. They indicate the direction we have chosen over many lives and the colours are stronger and more prominent than in the other two. (Hence the symbolic meaning of the Red Indian headdress when in ancient days they put different coloured feathers in different parts of the band to represent various accomplishments and heights of achievement. The feathers are a solidified aspect of those radiations.)

Beyond this, like a huge beacon which shines out into the night, is a radiation of pure light. Formed from energies from the cosmos, it radiates like a firework display. It is the externalization of the Christ experience. It is the golden halo of light depicted in religious paintings. Not, of course, like a flat pancake but rather like a three-dimensional dome. We all have a halo – these energies must radiate – but some are larger and brighter than others.

If in a past life or in more than one life we have chosen to go deeply into any kind of knowledge, we register this colour prominently and permanently in the crown. This energy will be so strong that it will radiate further then any other, and as it becomes fortified over successive lives, it will indicate the direction of the journey through our lives.

A colour in any other centre reflects our personality and a possible imbalance to be rectified. But in the top of the head it indicates an overall ability. It is a colour we have already worked through, a skill that we can call on at any time. Those in our centres reflect our current challenges and are colours to be eventually 'sent up' to the top.

On Earth we sense our place; in a hospital, a university, in an office. We segregate and choose according to our colour vibrations. Between incarnations, too, we inhabit a vibratory space, and part of us is in touch with these dimensions all the time. We go back to this space between lives but it is also an evolving space. In successive incarnations we are adding accomplishments and specializing more as we grow towards wisdom, and each time we go back we have raised our vibrations or added another one. Thus we enhance the long periods often spent between incarnations.

The more colours gathered at the top of the head through our incarnations, the more interesting and evolved we are. As we can see, we have far greater potential than we realize.

We each radiate three or four principal colours and this overall combination gives us the sense of who we are.

GOLD shows wisdom of the highest kind – a past in which we have lived a high monastic life. Here are the records of everything of importance in all religions and once we reach this dimension all religions are unified. To have gold means that we have acquired wisdom in previous lives and have a reservoir to use for our centres when necessary. Gold at the top of the head is rare. It points out the special ones who have totally transformed themselves and now hold the keys to universal consciousness.

WHITE shows we are working towards the brotherhood of men. It indicates a link between souls. Once we acquire white (and this means a past monastic life) we can be put under great strain and into situations of acute loneliness and survive. We will not commit suicide and have enormous recouperative strength. We have the ability for silence and to keep still.

PEACH shows a sequence of eight or twelve lives of service; depending on the shade of peach – chosen to build towards spirit. Each life dedicated to achievement of one virtue. It is a position of status, a mastership.

PEARL. Those who train on the peach ray may then go into the pearl dimension to train others through difficult lives.

DEEP PINK shows in those who are training to put people and ideas together. They are a link between this world and the next. It is the colour of spiritual love which blends and links together.

SILVER shows someone who is aware of things on a wider level and because of this awareness will come through difficult and different situations. Silver people have a special quality. They understand the right of every person to hold his own beliefs. They are universal people and often have a special job on earth.

STEEL GREY, a mix of white and black means judgement. Too much black means pessimism, too much white means optimism. In balance it produces the fair judgement characteristics of the judge. In our passage through time and space we must learn to judge with discrimination.

CREAM means investigation; lives in which we have added bits and pieces to our knowledge but not established anything too permanently. Cream people are professionals, possibly in some form of media, who need to meet and move.

As we return to the spectrum, we should remember that if these colours are established at the top of the head, they are an ability we already possess and can call upon.

MAGENTA. We all have a touch of this. It means a past life in which we were an administrator, and we are here again to administrate. Perhaps to organize groups of people.

VIOLET, as it radiates further, is any artistic pursuit; a painter, an actor a writer. A more pink violet is an organizing artist, a director.

INDIGO indicates a past life as a healer and if it appears in the triple crown we are probably now a doctor of some kind.

TURQUOISE means that lecturing will come easily.

BLUE indicates we are good at teaching but not necessarily at lecturing. We have a special way of relating to our pupils and the colour shows the kind of devotion necessary to make progress with another human being.

GREEN to excess in the other centres means we are too soft-hearted and over-generous. Here it is a positive sign and indicates a past life in which we had an affinity with the natural world. By tuning into nature we can sense what kind of food we need.

YELLOW means dedication to a chosen lifestyle; the achievement of some kind of college degree in a past life which has continued in this life as devotion to a profession or study.

ORANGE is rarely seen at the top of the head. Since it is to do with physical activity the soul may have evolved through some form of physical demonstration. Since it is also to do with food and productivity a farmer would also have orange at the top of the head.

RED the colour of evolution indicates a person who studies the mechanics of birth or is constructively helping us to understand the growth process better. Our present outlook is coloured, too, by the kinds of initiations we have had in the past, and these show up as the colour WINE at the top of the head. Red Indian initiations, for example, were painful – an indication that they were truly ready to step into another level of awareness. This may have been the case if you are impatient with other people's pain. On the other hand, if our initiation went wrong in some way, we may now be terrified of pain.

Colours cannot be classified too precisely. Each colour has hundreds of shades which may also be dirty or clean. Even the same colour can have different spiritual values, depending on which scale of light intensity it is. The art of seeing colour is very subtle. The colours themselves interpenetrate and affect each other all the time.

Most of us are only sensitive to the ordinary 'major scale' of colours. In psychic vision there are many scales of energy and colour – like the scales in music, filled with more and more light as the resonances reach higher and higher. There are colours, ranges of 'pure light' radiations above the head that even the best seers cannot comprehend in earthly terms.

CHAPTER THREE

Rose Pink: The Breath of God

Within the history of mankind and the history of the individual is the same pattern. We represent the microcosm and the macrocosm of experience. The same pattern of growth and change, for primitive man and for the primitive within each of us, seems set on a course towards refinement. As humanity has grown and refined through successive stages of evolution, so each one of us has refined through successive incarnations. As humanity is the product of its past, so we are the sum total of our past lives.

When a child is born, he carries the seeds of his personal past inside him and as he grows older the chakras will reflect the period in earthly terms that he has reached along the path. Each time we incarnate, according to what we have before birth chosen to learn, we add to our centres, which are the building blocks of our life. And as, during our life, we meet people with whom we have been corded on various centres in the past, these centres begin to function.

The age of seven is important for a child. Until then he is sensitive to the psychic but comparatively free from past life experience. He can cope with this sensing through the protection of his mother. If our colours 'run' when we are young and vulnerable, it is she who supplements us. We draw her energy to balance – sometimes to her detriment.

A pregnant woman often radiates deep blue – which is why the Virgin Mary wears a blue cloak in religious paintings – and this she can give to her unborn child. If then, after pregnancy, she cannot produce enough indigo, the child will often be ill during his young life. It is she who is depleted. When she is pregnant a woman will instinctively eat the right food, but once the child is born the instinct often fades and she may not replenish in the way she should. The fault lies in the whole modern birth process which is now so unnatural. After birth there is too little closeness between mother and child and it is the mother who loses in the end because her baby will be forced to finds its harmony in some other way.

Of course it takes two parents to provide the balance of energy we need to make our chakras shine. Small children are vulnerable. A baby who is not given love dies. But as we grow older we take less replenishment from our mother and father and more from the Sun. And once we begin to draw from other people and from the natural world, it is then that we become prone to illness. At around the age of seven, we begin to take responsibility for our own chakras and must adjust them accordingly during this period of transference. The more unbalanced our chakras, the more clinging we are as children. An outgoing child will produce his own inner stability, while an insular child fears his inner instincts and lives with a feeling of insecurity. He knows deep down there is something missing that he needs.

A child radiates pink, the spiritual colour of innocence, and until puberty the influence of past lives lies low. But as we begin to mature our colour vibrations grow denser and once we are sexual, ready to reproduce, the sexual area deepens to red. There is an opening of the psyche which puberty brings on. A child may experience poltergeists or telekinesis, and these are signs that past life experiences are reawakening. This is the poignant and possibly dangerous age when a child, for no apparent reason, may go off the rails. He may be drawn into remnants of a past life and often in the negative. One life more than others may jump out to the surface.

At this psychic teen age, the Third Eye begins to function more acutely, which in some cases may cause mental disturbance. But generally children by this time are using the rational side of their brains and anything that strikes them as 'odd' will be pushed into the background and explained through logic. Often, the more psychic the child, the more he will base himself in the analytical side of his nature. Aware deep down of his psychic nature, he will choose not to admit it or bring it out. He will prefer to concentrate on the usual.

For most people the Third Eye is protected by seven veils – hence the dance of the seven veils – which represent the seven chakras, and until the veils are dissolved we cannot 'see'. Only when each centre is sufficiently strong to cope with the experience will the veils diminish, like a mist: and then not in any sequence but as they naturally go. For direct access to past lives of our own or of other people, our centres must be all fully open and the veils withdrawn. Then we will have access to a deeper chamber of knowledge.

When a veil disperses, it can disperse a little or more, so there are also seven grades of dispersal. A block can stop the dispersing altogether which means we have to deal with our inner life, but providing all the veils come off then a different type of third eye appears. When all the coarse etheric levels disappear it becomes much more translucent and beautiful. It is as though a door is bolted to protect the treasure but a certain key will unlock that treasure which can be taken out and used.

All knowledge we possess is there, even universal knowledge. To enter into the deepest aspects of this other mind leaves no doubt that there is a Creator. Without that link we would not exist.

The Third Eye should show blue, which indicates our primitive, animal ability to tune into what is going on in other places and other realities. Additional flashes of silver show our own refinement of this area. But it should also show yellow (often with gold in an advanced human being) and this indicates our ability to use these gifts. The Third Eye is our balance between the rational and the non-rational.

By the time we have had an unhappy love affair – and most people do have them – we will have begun to carve a path into the psyche. The Third Eye will have a chance to open because it is our sensitivity to the people around us that provokes the third eye to function. The more life crashes around us, the more we will open into past lives, and the more we can begin to understand the law of karma.

The law of karma says that we receive from life exactly what we have paid in. As ye sow, so shall ye reap. If, from past lives, there is unfinished business or an unfinished relationship, we must at some point fulfill that destiny. And as we progress we might consciously realize that certain people have come into this present life through past life experience. There are debts to pay and rewards to reap. Once we accept that each of us is aiming for a goal, over many lifetimes, we will understand that unhappy moments are part of a learning process, an opening out. When we begin to know this we can begin to know our own needs, physically, mentally, emotionally and spiritually.

To be hurt and rejected by someone is part of a 'bargain' between our souls. A relationship begins and ends when it is right, because we are never hurt by strangers. It is our purpose on earth to grow and although we do not recognize them as such, it is our friends from past lives who are there to help. They are corded to us from birth.

And as all these experiences from different lives have brought through progressive changes in the colours which emanate from our bodies, so mankind in general has progressed. Primitive man was centred in the lower chakras of the body. He needed the potential aggression and anger of those denser vibrations to utilize the militant aspects of his nature. The red energy was needed to procreate, and the hunger of orange centre to move into action. He was psychic but his brain was not yet fully developed.

As the yellow mind centre began to evolve, man was able to sense the appropriateness of his gifts and learn to use them, and with each successive growth humanity has been developing towards a higher level. Each individual is working towards an awareness of a 'higher self', a greater wisdom, and this can only happen when the lower energies of the body are brought up to energize a dormant part of the brain.

White has always been the mark of a celibate. It is the High Priest colour. By being celibate the ancient yogis allowed the white vibration into the reproductive centre. The negative qualities of the sexual area disappeared, leaving its warmth but not its passion. By overlaying the red with white the area became spiritual pink and with this sort of control the energies were raised for higher things. The basic sex energy is necessary for the propagation of the species, but as the soul evolves this same energy can be transmuted to vibrate more finely.

Those who have had a past life as a priest or monk have the automatic potential to bring in white. (The soul may choose such a life in order to work in isolation but without fear of loneliness. When vibratory rates are changing there is always a need for some kind of withdrawal. Certain things must be done undercover and in silence. There is nothing more lonely than a seed in the ground.) The ancient yogis on the other hand, by living alone and performing exercises of concentration, will power and breathing, produce this transmutation through conscious austerity. But unless the colour is already registered in the Third Eye, it is difficult to raise the red energy up the spine in safety, and those who indulge in the psychic practice of 'raising the kundalini' before it is ready to happen automatically, are courting danger. Unless the basement energy is already pink, it is easy to manipulate the sexual energy in the wrong way, and to experience these gifts before we are ready is often to get more than we bargained for.

But whether it is a natural part of evolution or a conscious effort, our aim should be to dissolve some of the heat from the sexual centre. Pink is the colour which unites. It is the colour of mediumship. In pink we come between nature and those who want to destroy our heritage. We mediate between Man and God; the sky and the earth; the highest and the lowest. Once we love God and our neighbour, the first of God's commandments, the rest will automatically follow.

Gradually, then, through different lives we learn how to control our instincts and grow towards an awareness of the intuition. A tool to be used by a bright, clean and alert mind. Thus the old mysteries can be used with new awareness. That is our legacy and our future.

This is obviously an over-simplification of an extraordinarily complex pattern of growth through the history of mankind and also within each individual. A growth pattern that emerges through all past lives but is also replicated in one particular lifetime. We can recognize the process of humanity as we begin to realize more and more what is happening in our own personal evolution. We can express this process in terms of colour.

There is imbalance in the world today, between people who live in the mind and who analyze to the point where nothing psychic can penetrate. Whose rational understanding completely blocks any ability to produce the gifts we all once had. On the other hand there are those who negate the intellect in the extreme and think that to learn or study is to lose the psychic gift. These people rely on intuition and chanelled wisdom and do not realize that by leaning so heavily on past knowledge and past lives, they are not using the most precious weapon we have, the mind.

Ultimately, when we can centre between the two in the green of the heart – a combination of the psychic blue and the mind yellow – the balance will allow us to feel towards psychic knowledge with the heart but to use the brain to avoid being fooled. It is man's heritage to be part of nature and part of every other human being and by joining these two centres we can make a 'leap' into a higher principle. The principle of light or spirit.

As humanity as a whole and each of us individually rises from the red towards the green, we are changing our rate of vibration. Our colours become lighter and more ethereal as we refine our energies from the gross to the spiritual. And in doing so, it becomes inevitable that we must change our attitude to life. As we become centred in the green heart area, this green becomes more gentle. Gradually it will infuse with its opposite, the spiritual shade of pink. The red of the base chakra will have transmuted into pink. And since these changes will register in the third eye, this too will show signs of rose pink. In a higher initiate it can even go towards a violet colour.

As the 'higher mind' comes into play, the third eye itself will change. On the old level we keep all the effects of our past lives within us. They are there to be integrated and thus overcome. Once we reach this deeper level we register only the aspects of each life that are useful for attaining our goals. We begin to sense when things are right and wrong. We achieve a deeper knowing from a greater depth. We have thrown out all the irrelevant emotions and illnesses that bound us to the daily round and kept only the mind qualities we need to take us on.

We are all, each human being, composed of seven bodies. Five more beside the physical and etheric. Bodies invisible, except through clairvoyant sight since they too vibrate at increasingly high rates as they progress more finely towards the spiritual aspects of our nature. The higher vibratory bodies are fed with cosmic rays and sustain a life of their own. When, for example, we sense a change in atmosphere in a room, it means that a different etheric dimension is being felt by our consciousness. One of our other bodies is gaining predominance over the mundane body and tuning into its own dimension. In that dimension it will tune into everything that goes on there.

Each body has a dimension in which a tangible world exists. 'In my father's house there are many mansions.' Each body belongs not only to one mansion which everyone shares, but to the mansion of its own particular vibratory rates. Obviously the highest body is closest to all the other bodies, but each in between is slightly different and will share with all others on that level. It is easier to imagine that parts of us are living elsewhere. Events happen on very subtle levels and are then 'pulled through the ethers' into 'reality', but sometimes although our soul knows what it wants, our body consciousness may negate it. Until our body can be persuaded away from what it thinks and wants, the higher bodies cannot come through.

Our three highest bodies correspond to a more highly developed sense of spirit and comprise colours which cannot yet be described in earthly terms, other than that they are 'ethereal'. There are colours inside us that are not Earth colours and have a brightness not of this Earth. As mankind evolves so the other bodies have come into play and as we return to a sense of spirit so they will be used more and more.

Each body reacts to the next and there is a constant passing of information from one to the other. If one is out of balance this affects the rest. If we take drugs, for example, this will show on the etheric body as well as on the physical. And to add even more complications, each of our bodies may also be affected, each one differently, according to karmic experience. We may have a contaminated etheric body from past misuse – which may explain why some people can smoke a great deal and remain healthy while others contract lung cancer.

Over the centuries we build our structure according to past lives. We earn our seven bodies. If someone is slightly impure in the etheric body and instinctively lives a good life to purify that body, the impurities will seep into the physical body and be released completely. Suffering on this earth – which is karma – and death from such diseases as cancer, may sometimes be explained in that we cannot lose all of the ugly aspects from the other bodies. As we become more pure and closer to God, some of the 'sickness' will penetrate our physical body. This has to be cleared out and released. If the body cannot do this it will become sick and die, which again may explain why so many 'good' people seem to suffer so badly. It should also be said that some people do choose to come to earth simply for other people's growth and may become invalids for this purpose.

A discipline such as yoga may clear the body of its current physical problems, but once the body is purified this leaves space for anything else that needs help. It can link with the other bodies and work on negativity there. It can infiuence the mind and emotions to change negative patterns. Our ambition should be for a freer, healthier flow between the bodies so the mind may be left free for the job it should be doing and that is, to project thought positively.

But it is the physical body that is our main vehicle on earth and if we can have true feeling for this one body, then the rest must automatically follow. It is our first duty to love and protect our physical body because it is this that influences the rest. This is the reason we are drawn to earth, for it is only through the physical body that the toxins can be released from the other bodies in the form of illness. Only the physical body can make up the debts of past lives. Impurities are condensed into matter and eliminated from the body – which is why the yogis were so concerned about constipation! By releasing these toxins into the earth, we can see what an important role she plays. The closer we are to the earth, the more nurturing the 'Mother' can be. It is she, through her magnetic force, who fosters our transmutation and change.

The more positive and clean our physical body, the more clearly our other bodies may shine. If the front line of soldiers drops to the ground the rest of the regiment will be disoriented, so if the first of our bodies is unstable the rest are vulnerable. We cannot hurt one without hurting the others. It is a question of balance.

So our attitude to the human body should be one of reverence. It is wrong to ignore its beauty and value and to think it ugly. It is our duty to know the vehicle within which we are making our journey on earth. As every part of a car must be in working order to run smoothly, so the body, too, must work in all its inter-related parts before it can become whole. The centres must be kept in harmony. Firstly through exercise but also through BREATHING. For it is breath that gives our earthly body its stability. We can live without water for some time and without food for even longer. But we cannot live without breathing.

But breathing has a far greater significance than we normally realize. God took a breath when he created the world and He has been taking breaths ever since. Everything in the universe breathes. Each in its own way and each with its own vehicle for breath. Human beings breathe, animals breathe, plants breathe. The chakras breathe, the Third Eye breathes. The Earth itself breathes with almost a 'cosmic' breath. The earth reacts to other planets in the universe and within that magnetic attraction is a kind of breathing.

Each of our bodies breathes. As the physical body breathes with lungs, so the other bodies have organs for breath. When the yogis perform non-breathing, they stop the lungs and centre on breath coming into the other bodies. Yoga breathing made the body strong but in a wider sense, by tapping cosmic fields of knowledge, it is also helped the yogis to receive a form of enlightenment.

The ancients aspired to being in tune on a cosmic scale and to alignment with the stars. In meditation they would take a breath to a star and imagine the star giving breath back. In this way they sensed the outer and inner coming to life. The in and the out. The in-breath and the out-breath. We are part of the cosmos and our bodies depend on the cosmos to be fed. The reality of God is in the in- and out-breath.

We breathe in different ways, according to our colour pattern. 'By their breathing shall ye know them'! Violet people, for example, are likely to be shallow breathers because they are emotional and artistic. While red (the outgoing) and orange (the sporty) people will tend to take deeper breaths to boost the lower chakras. And it is probably the yellow people who breathe least effectively. Hunched over books or the office desk they will tend to take shallow breaths. They will have less vitality and be easily depleted. Continuous bad breathing has a destructive effect on the chakras because they are unable to clear themselves.

The breath itself is coloured since the ethers are coloured and we continuously breathe into ourselves the colours of the people, the places and objects around us. If someone is depressed, for example, or has been smoking, they will breathe out grey or brown and their dirt is superimposed on on to our centres. On top of that, each centre also accumulates negativity by thoughts and actions. So if our in-breath is good, but the out-breath too shallow, we will accumulate negativity which the body must eliminate. We should aim to breathe in the colours we need and breathe out the dark, dirty colours we are not using.

So the condition of our centres depends on the quality of our breath. From ancient days the lungs have been recognized as our entrance to spirutuality. It is far easier for us to change the breath than to change the circulation – a far more advanced task.

We can tune into our breathing. Even if we do not know the colours we need we may take it for granted – because we do not feel full of energy – that our breath needs improving. If we then increase both the in-breath and out-breath and tell ourselves we are going to do this until our breath is as fresh and pink as a young child's, we are tuning into ourselves. We will then find we reach a sudden point at which there is actually a change in the breath itself. At the moment we actually feel different we then know it will be useful to breathe in various colours.

We often feel instinctively when we have a lack of some colours inside us. When we feel blue and depressed and heavy we know we need bright vibrant happy colours. When we are het up, hot and angry we can now we need cool, beautiful blues to cool us down. When we are cooped up in an office and badly need the countryside we can breathe in green. A person who does this actually changes the colour which come out of his mouth; he changes the colour of his room.

We should aim for a deep natural in-breath and a long, smooth out-breath. But on the whole most of us breathe incorrectly and most of us are depleted by it. By learning to breathe correctly we can heal ourselves. By breathing into a specific part of our body changes can occur. We have the seeds of rightness within us and by breathing properly we can improve not only the physical body but the other bodies too. The deeper the in-breath and the better the out-breath, the cleaner and stronger the chakras. There are many types of breathing but if we are to take breathing seriously, especially deep breathing, we must give it some thought. With so much pollution we should try to take deep breaths early in the morning when the air is cleaner and the out-breath can be a real purification.

We should remember, too, that thoughts are vibrations and what we imagine can cause a stirring in the atmosphere. We can 'touch' areas of the body with our minds. If we think of the kidneys we set up an internal vibration like an invisible hand which actually touches them. To be healthy we have to be imaginative. But in order to be effectively imaginative we must have a healthy outlook on life.

If we think that 'there is always something wrong with my kidneys', the fear will emanate as a sickly yellow colour and this will vibrate throughout the body. To constantly complain to gain other people's sympathy, is to kill ourselves off. The more we talk about an illness the more it is emphasized.

Concentrating on an area changes that area. So we must breathe with the imagination and we can begin to think of healing the body in terms of breathing. Remember, however, that the area in which the disease is manifest is not necessarily the seat of the illness. Disease may manifest through related organs. A heart attack, for example, may be due to dirty blood or kidneys that cannot cope with toxins (perhaps through smoking or drinking). So at the same time we need awareness of a destructive lifestyle.

No one should try to influence the kind of breathing that comes naturally to us. If we have not used our lungs properly for years it would be wrong to lengthen or hold the breath in a way we find too difficult. To begin with, practise breathing gently. We are changing a lifetime of bad habits and this must be done slowly.

As a general rule, pumping breath moves the chakras faster, a slow breath moves the chakras slower, and as we advance, the breaths we practise depend on the state of our energies; whether too large or too small, whether open or dirty. But to begin, most of us need to eliminate some kind of negativity, smoking, drinking, over-eating, drugs, too much coffee and strong tea, negative emotions and thoughts or simply bad out-breaths.

Practise a simple *cleansing breath*. Either sitting cross-legged, standing or kneeling, bring the body forward from the waist on the out-breath and empty as much as possible.

Another simple exercise is the yoga *complete or basic breath*. If your stomach protrudes, this probably means you do not breathe well. If your out-breath is too shallow your stomach and rib cage muscles will loosen, so we should aim to make our out-breath twice as long before starting this exercise.

Never begin a breathing exercise without stretching. Elongate in the waist and try not to slip back so the stomach will not be extended on the in-breath. Breath should lengthen the spine so whenever you take a breath, touch the ceiling with your imagination. (In doing this do not raise the shoulders, although it is useful to take a couple of breaths a day in which you do raise the shoulders and bring more air into the higher parts of the lungs.) If at first you cannot sit straight, use a chair or a wall.

Breathe in slowly throught the nostrils, filling first the lower part of the lungs to bring the diaphragm into play. As this descends it will push forward the front walls of the abdomen and give the organs a gentle squeeze. The navel should stay firm or raised very little. Fill the middle part of the lungs, pushing out the ribs, breast bone and chest. Then fill the highest part of the lungs, lifting the upper chest. In this final movement, the lower abdomen will draw in again slightly to give the lungs support and help to fill the top of the lungs. Try to make the breath continuous and uniform.

Then exhale, reversing the process. Hold the chest in a firm position and draw the abdomen in a little, lifting it upward slowly as the air leaves the lungs.

Our nostrils emit different colours. The right nostril is associated with the sun, the left with the moon; one warming with reds and orange colours, the other cooling, with blue or violet. Hence an indication of balance and harmony is also in the colour of the lungs. We should be wary of how we pollute them.

Alternate nostril breathing. This breath clears the nasal passages and helps the nerves since it rocks the chakras and pacifies them. Sit with the spine erect, eyes closed. Place the right thumb against the right nostril and press to close. Breathe in slowly through the left nostril for as long as comfortable. Close both nostrils for a moment by closing the left nostril with the ring and little finger. Lift the thumb and breathe out slowly through the right nostril. Now breathe in through the right nostril, close both for a moment and again breathe our slowly through the left. Continue for as long as you wish. As we progress we begin to know intuitively what we need.

A warning about holding the breath. This slows down the chakras and increased the carbon dioxide level which causes a slight dilation of the blood vessels and improves circulation within the brain. Although this makes us calmer and more aware, it can be harmful if we then do a yoga shoulder stand or bend the head downward because we have removed the safety factor which stops too much blood going to the brain. Those with a weak heart or blood pressure should not hold the breath.

Finally, we may breathe to recharge. By breathing in and out deeply and slowly with the hands and feet locked together, we find strength. To help the energies flow, take a breath around the body. Take the in-breath up the right side of the body and the out-breath down the left side. Then breathe up the left side and down the right to balance. Breathe up the front of the body and down the back, then up the back and down the front so the whole body feels covered. Continue this exercise until both hands tingle.

Gold: Wisdom of the Gods

Most of us know deep down where things are going wrong; we can sense which centres are not functioning well. Conversely we can usually tell when our energies are gathering strength; when we can trust our intuition and the mind feels less tired and depleted; when the throat is free of germs and we keep colds at bay; when we can allow ourselves to fall in love but not be destroyed if the relationship goes wrong; when the digestions works well and the reproductive area is naturally alive. These are the signs of growing strength and balance. And at the point where all these things make us feel completely alive and healthy, we are probably ready for a deeper learning.

If a stone is dropped into a pool, it will ripple out in small vibratory waves. If a stone is then dropped onto each separate ripple, these too will make ripples of their own. They are small vibrating energy spots. In the chakra, if it rotates sufficiently fast, minute invisible points in the ripple sprinkle out like stars and this energy moves up and down and round, like tiny fountains. When these fountains scatter all over each other they look like huge coloured jewels and it is then, in the ideal, that the centres are ready for OPENING.

To open a chakra is to feel at one with that centre, and with the heart centre in particular there is a sense of being everywhere, of floating; as though opening the arms in joy and returning to the moment of creation. The centres are our pathlines to eternity. To the Resurrection. Any form of excitement and pleasure will open a chakra slightly, such as watching children at play or being in league with animals and nature. Love will open a chakra and so will imagination, but then it will close again. The purpose of yoga is eventually to be able to open the chakras wide. And the more we are in control of this opening, the more control we have of shutting them again and that is important too. The stronger the centres become and the more mobile, the wider they can open in safety.

Opening happens when the fountains of energy push out of the centre and draw back to what appears to be a hole. The wider the chakras can open the greater the space for cosmic energy to come in, which brings a change in vibratory rates and a conscious shift in awareness. And once the chakras open to the limit, the colours of the other bodies can then shine through; they will flow into the space. When all the chakras are open we then have the ability to heal.

In opening, we experience the 'outer' energy of the cosmos coming through us, not only the energies which rise from the base chakra to the top of the head as before. When the energies are strong, we are also much closer to our Third Eye and to the possibility of psychic awareness, because the forehead too is strong. It is often said that God is within and we should try to look inward. But the Third Eye breathes in and out and when this is open it closes us to the God experience within. We become aware of the God outside. In fact we should appreciate both because life is a matter of balance.

In realizing we have not only one short life, but an eternity ahead of us, we are open to a cosmic outlook — to know that we each have a groove, a job of our own to do of relevance to the cosmos. And as the 'higher mind' body begins to shine through and we work more calmly on those chakras, these centres begin to radiate a golden quality. Like alchemists we are working towards gold; towards being golden human beings. As we progress we become capable of golden moments in our lives. We give a golden glow that is experienced as something precious by the people who come into our lives.

The higher mind is like a golden flower and golden people are part of cosmic consciousness. It is the Christ consciousness, in which the only way to give back to God, who possesses everything, is to pass on something to someone else. In this way we repay God for our life. By this time in our awakening, we too possess all, for this higher body allows in the more spiritual aspects of our nature. When the chakras are open we are opening up to the wiser parts of our being which can be used for other people. Healing is giving people what they need in whichever way they need it.

Gold means a freedom few people understand. The law of karma ceases to exist since a golden person needs nothing. He cannot be corded to anyone and no-one can lean on him; there are no projections or attachments. He is completely happy within himself and love is given with no expectation or demand.

Of course, to open all the chakras and heal, to be in touch with the cosmos is the ideal. But the ideal seldom occurs. Nobody is perfect. We are all conditioned by the kind of life we have lived and also by our past lives, and usually there is a great deal lacking in us.

The path towards opening should follow a progressive strengthening of the mind. To exercise as in yoga, for example without thought might open further a chakra that is already too open, and not touch another that is too tightly closed. Yoga is a powerful force — more powerful than even many yoga teachers realize.

Chakras of the less sophisticated ancients were far smaller and did not merge one into the other. A disciple came to his master with a clean set of chakras. Away from his family and uncorded to anyone, he would follow a spiritual path to gain access to his own wisdom. With the elimination of the sex act he transmuted his centres. This was done through exercise in concentration, by not talking during meals, by confining the flow of thought; by no emotional involvement and tuning into nature, by talking only about things confined to the spiritual path, by tuning into the Master and concentrating on the Third Eye.

The centres were charged by holding each yoga posture for a long time and once they were conquered the sexual area was then boosted to send energy to the top of the head. With all the centres open, cosmic light could come through and initiation was complete. Long held postures were stopped except to keep a centre alive.

'Initiation', part of the human legacy, is open to anyone. We can come to higher consciousness by overcoming weakness through the tests we all encounter in life. Discipline is vital, but Eastern techniques are no longer always necessary. We may chant and go through the motions of ancient dance; we may still use incense and candles and wear certain robes in a religious ceremony, but we no longer need these rituals. All these things are now *within us*. We only externalize them when we are vulnerable or when we want to impress something deeply on another person.

In the future ritual will be minimal. We are now moving into a new age, where within an instant we can bring about the necessary change in consciousness. We have been weaned from the beginning of time. We have been learning how to find our own potential.

Sometimes, when people have been working on themselves or practising yoga, for example, for some time, they discover they can heal and will do so because they want to be applauded. Today there are many such people, who fall into the trap of assuming they have gifts that most people do not experience, and try to use them to gain some kind of power. On the other hand, there are others who do the opposite, who run away from their responsibility and continually run themselves down. When a person has 'collected' potential through many lives, he then has to make a choice; to use it or not. Some people have their pot of gold, but cannot seem to see it is there.

But someone who rushes into healing may suddenly become ill and wonder why, and it must be reiterated that to work effectively on someone else, all the centres – channels – used to transmit cosmic energy must be open. To heal before you are ready, before your understanding has grown sufficiently, could bring on a heart attack or cancer, and it will almost certainly damage those chakras which are not yet opened.

Without knowledge of what is happening, healing can be dangerous. Not least because in certain circumstances healing someone may be wrong. Illness may be a karmic condition that has to be worked through. To be approached is fine; people may be drawn to you to be helped. But to seek them out because you want to heal is wrong. Healing before the chakras are properly opened will hurt your own body and also give the wrong insight into when someone else needs healing.

The idea, as we have said, is to heal with all the centres open, but it is worth seeing what happens if we heal when one or other of the chakras remains closed.

Closed Chakras

If the *base* chakra is closed, the energies coming in from the cosmos from the top of the body are stopped before they reach the basement and a great deal of energy bounces off the red centre. There will be an attempt to boost that area because the chakras of the other bodies work on white light and this one cannot. People in this position are often drawn to sex books or love stories or even to pornographic films. Sex itself will revive the area to some extent but if this is lacking the energy needed to heal will be drawn from the etheric body. This depletion will cause illness in the reproductive area.

If the *digestive* centre cannot open, then energies from the top of the head will hit the stomach. If the base chakra is also closed this centre will be quite safe, but the stomach itself will degenerate through constant bombardment of energy. If, however, the bottom chakra is open and receptive, the problem is worse. There is a huge suction from the basement and as the energy hits the stomach it is pulled through into the base chakra. This could cause diseases as dangerous as cancer.

When the *mind* chakra remains closed, but those below and above are open, then the energy bombardment from above is very strong. If it hits the mind centre and is drawn into the two open centres beneath, the energy moves so fast that a healer will find his mind affected in some way. Instead of feeling open and clean he will sense a slight dizziness and his memory may be impaired. In this case it is better that the bottom two centres are closed so the energy will hit the mind more gently.

Vibrations from the cosmos can only accumulate around an open centre. If, for example, the heart centre is closed the cosmic green ray cannot come through. Instead the healer must use his own etheric green ray, to his detriment. The heart is often one of the most difficult areas to open, which is why some healers have died of heart attack. If in this or past lives the heart has been in emotional turmoil it will want to hold together for as long as possible. An open heart centre brings great understanding and love in a universal sense. When the heart chakra does open it often happens in great pain but once those energies are working positively, there is a clear channel. This is why some people need unhappiness in their lives before that channel will appear and be ready for opening.

When the heart opens to the cosmos for healing, the colour which shines through is pink – the sign of cosmic love. In healing, if the energies coming from the cosmos hit a closed heart centre the energies shoot round in a circle. This is felt like a hit in the heart and may manifest in a small heart attack. If the lower three centres are open, pulling the energies down, the affect of this suction is even stronger. So the feelings in the heart depend on which of the chakras beneath are open and how much energy is being pulled through.

If all the lower four chakras are open and the throat shut, the energies going into the throat will produce throat trouble and colds. At the same time you would not be a competent healer. If the forehead does not open then in any case you could not heal.

The opening of the chakras is a journey towards God, and unless there is love to keep the spiritual aspects of the heart open to other people they will not stay open.

However, some chakras can open, not in the spirit of love and this is most dangerous. Chakras can be opened through the force of sex by 'swirling' through all forms of perversion which has no outward manifestation in love of mankind. Arrogance, vanity, anger and passion will move the chakras and produce strong psychic powers. At first such practices may feel good as the energies spin wildly. You may have fun for several years, but then the very act of what you are doing will turn sour. There is a moment of saturation of negative energies and someone who looked beautiful at thirty-five will begin to deteriorate. 'By their fruits shall ye know them.' If at any time a chakra becomes dirty it will automatically begin to close.

Once the mind decides it has finished healing, the healing stops automatically. In the same way as we have an automatic digestive system, this too is an automatic process. However, as with all automatic processes, it works far better if we are aware of their function and consciously contribute to their well-being. The tiny points of energy are attracted to each other and can draw back together again to be covered by the jewels.

As we become more aware, the other bodies radiate through and the centres become more full of light. The coarse etheric colours begin to disintegrate and although the colours will be the same as before, they will be on a higher ethereal level. Then the golden aspect too can come through. It does happen that vibrations from other bodies will, by a similar learning process, come through without the chakras opening. Not actively engaged in any form of healing we may not need the extra energies for ourselves. In the process of change there can be disturbances as the coarser energies move away and the more mystical chakras appear.

There must, of course, be slight changes in personality and outlook. The body, our vehicle of expression has been expressing itself through various colour vibrations, and as these begin to change all our organs must adjust and this adjustment goes right through the body. We may even fall ill at this point if some accumulated dirt in the etheric body returns to the physical body for elimination.

We may wonder why someone who lives a debauched life gets away with things, while another beautiful person is always in trouble. This happens because those with coarser ethers have a storage space for their negativity. If they were to try to become more spiritually aware, they would go through intense suffering because the accumulated dirt in the etheric would move to the body to be cleansed. Those who have shed the coarser ethers and now experience instant karma often have nowhere for their negativity to go and the smallest action affects them immediately. If they are also helping others to clean up their ethers, they have a double burden.

In a few people the centres are left permanently open, to constantly transmit light. And as we have said, they must adjust to a 'new' body and new consciousness. They 'no longer stain the white radiance of eternity'. But it is important to realize that even in opening there are different qualities to that opening. And transmission always depends on the quality of the instrument. We may be capable of opening but still not be perfect healers.

To heal properly we must be capable of opening to the core, the very centre of all the centres, where we meet the double hole phenomenon of outer space (the microcosm of the macrocosm). The black hole, facing other planes, takes in energy and channels it into the chakra itself where it is manifested through the white hole. It is interesting to note that a seer who goes deeply into the channel can see the obstructions which we now call 'blocks'. As a child grows, this channel grows with him and if from conception or at any later point there is a blockage then this will affect his health pattern.

The channels are also affected by genetic characteristics and illnesses of parents and grandparents. We may be born with blocks, and the soul – which does not commit itself to the body until the child is about to be born – must accept the blocks, be aware of them and at certain stages in its life try to remove them in some way. The body is like a secondhand car. When we accept a body we accept all the negativities of our ancestors. As with a secondhand car, we must look at the mechanics to see that it functions well enough to take us right through life. Whether or not we have chosen this malfunctioning to learn a lesson, we have to overcome it in some way. We all have the ability and courage to do so.

During healing, a healer's breathing will automatically change and he will automatically relax. Under tension the chakras remain closed, so if we want to open at all we must learn to relax, to empty the mind and be free to collect any cosmic vibrations we are worthy of receiving.

Relaxation

Relaxation prepares the body to release negativity. To lie still and relax is to tune more fully into the energy fields of the body and, more important, those of the earth and the cosmos. It is a going back to the source; an experience of being totally in harmony. We transfer our negativity into the earth to be absorbed, and can raise our spirit and our colours higher.

For deep relaxation it is best to have loosened the negative energies first through exercise. With exercise the circulation will improve and the system will be alive and alert, so that immobile and hard energies will have moved in various directions to be ready for release.

For relaxation lie in darkness in a place away from draughts. A dark room will help to raise our level of awareness. Cover the body with something light. Mose people, through bad posture, hold on to muscles that need not be used at all, which needlessly use up energy from food. The point of relaxation is to release the movement of the muscle structure from the body. By tuning into the releasing of any association with movement, we release the need for any outward expression. We must try to link up all the energies in the body and this cannot be fully achieved if we only relax, say, the toes or the knees. We must try to make not simply little pools of relaxation, but a full ocean into which we can dive and become conscious of the body.

So, beginning with the bottom of the body, when we tune into the feet we must try to pour the mind into them. Not just to dissolve them but to allow that feeling to be experienced throughout the whole body. At that second, with the feet relaxed, the whole body will be in tune with that feeling of the feet.

If this is done throughout the whole body we will sense a linking of energies through the body and eventually there will be no need to go right through the body. With no one part isolated from the rest, by relaxing the hands the whole body will relax simultaneously. And the areas which are relaxed can put their sense of calm into areas which for some reason may suddenly tense up.

During relaxation the chakras often slow down, especially those which are overcharged and the calmer you become the easier it is to enjoy relaxation. People with undercharged chakras may relax to the point where they automatically fall asleep. This may mean that the centres are not ready for action and nature has stopped the possibility of a different awareness.

But other people will be aware during relaxation that their body is calm, their centres are spinning softly and their mind is gently alive and alert. These people are ready for a new understanding.

Two people may be equally tense but their spiritual evolution different. One person may simply learn to relax to enjoy more fully his ordinary life. The other, however, may learn to relax and find suddenly that colours are coming through by themselves. The breath automatically changes and indigo, violet, blue or white light stream into his vision. He will know then that the path he has chosen in life will not be easy but he will know too that he must utilize some of these gifts that are beginning to come through.

Meditation opens us to something more universal and it should be approached with this kind of feeling. It is opening the door to self-awareness and should be seen as a positive experience, not an escape. It is a time to empty the mind, yet a time to concentrate. The room you choose to mediate in should feel good and comfortable. As we have said, plants, books, objects, painting all radiate their own vibrations and if you do not feel at ease with them they may be wrong for you. Meditate on an empty stomach and feel as free as possible from emotion so you may open to the depths your soul requires.

We give here a few ideas for your mind to follow, but remember that meditation is never the same experience for any two people. It is a journey of our own being. Sit in a position you can maintain without stress. The spine should be erect. Do not wear anything too tight.

We are conditioned to be slaves of time and this is something we want to overcome in meditation. Imagine a golden clock and spin it with your mind until it becomes a shining ball. Sense yourself moving out of this moment into a universal, cosmic beat.

Imagine you are a child of the universe, no longer tied to time, flowing in the sea of eternal rhythm and breath. You are the pulsations of the macrocosm of which this planet earth is a part. Gaze on the earth from above, see the radiations descending from the cosmos and the radiations coming up from the earth. Imagine the bands of energy around the earth. See the planet trying to evolve with you.

Bring the highest mountains into view, their whiteness like white light reflecting the sun. Try to feel in you their silence and splendour. You as a whole mountain of silence, majesty and beauty.

Then visualize the trees. See their glowing radiance and grow into them. Let your own radiations dig deeply into the earth; we too have roots like them. The trees cast off their old leaves and we can cast off old habits and bring our own renewal. We, too, come into bud and flower into new ideas and thoughts. We can bear the fruits of spirituality.

Look at the rivers and see the energy of water. Since we are comprised mostly of water, we are able to balance the liquids in our body. Try to feel the baptism of purification that water gives and tune into the blue of water.

Look at the people and send them a rose pink ray of love. Look at your own body and see it as a work of art. Your many auras and pulsating multi-coloured chakras, the soft flow of energy channels. Turn towards the golden side of your nature and become aware of the sun disk in you which gathers gold. See the sun radiating its warmth into you. Then visualize the moon in you, the feminine aspect, gentle and soft, dipping into silver. The deep blue sky with its splendour of stars.

Think of yourself as the microcosm, listen to the movement of your atoms. God gives us orange energy to eat and absorb food, but think of the food of the mind. Tune into ideas, make them violet and spiritual. Think of the food of the soul and feel your body receiving translucent light; channel it through all the centres purifying, cleansing and charging.

Then offer thanks for it all. Form wings of joy to fly towards the deeper level of awareness. Melt into the omnisience of the spirit. When you touch upon the immeasurable there are no words, no thoughts — just silence.

Although we must lose such heights of joy, it is always there inside us. We are WHITE LIGHT.

Negativity

Our aim is to make the energies bright and it is this brightness that produces jewel-like structures over the centres. These allow them, at the right time, to open in safety. But while the centres are still working towards balance, they radiate not jewels, but a number of different colours. And if the energies are overlaid with any negative colours, yoga is an ideal way to push them out.

BROWN is often said to mean greed and selfishness; the sign of an unpleasant character. But it should be seen more correctly as a stage at which we withdraw. If, for example, we have been hurt or have shown the outside world a side of us of which we are ashamed, we will say things that sound ugly or hurtful, or produce aggression that wants to destroy even the person we love most. But this is not the real us at all. We are simply saving ourselves from destruction or from other people's interference by withdrawing. We need to radiate brown as part of the phase we are going through.

BROWN, the colour of monkhood, in other chakras usually means RETREAT.

BROWN in general indicates a staleness of the energies, but more so in the RED reproductive centre and this is very common. The energies here need to be reactivated. We may live in the permissive age, but relatively few people are living lives of sexual fulfillment. The red area often retreats after an unhappy love affair; the energy becomes cloistered.

Masturbation, too, contrary to modern thinking, produces negative energies. It may stir up the base chakra, which is useful if the energy there is too hot and has no other outlet, but the energy could be used far more constructively – in helping other people or studying. Then, instead of feeling withdrawn and miserable when someone new comes along, the energy can be used more wisely.

In masturbation there is no exchange of energies. You will either tune into another person without their permission and by doing so interfere with their well-being because the stronger your mind, the more it will touch that person. And depending on how strong their protective instinct is, this will adversely affect their energy fields.

Or you will tune inwards, and by tuning into your own being you lose energy, which is counter-productive. Throughout our lives we should be completely in charge of all our energies. The object lesson in yoga is to be in charge of everything we are. It is our duty to clear not only our own energies but, being part of a whole, those of everyone else. If every human being works constructively towards being a 'glow', then the whole universe may be raised in consciousness.

Negative sex energies can also be used positively to open to the mystical side of our nature. An unhappy love affair can produce the kind of withdrawal needed to boost the meditative side of life, and once this is set in motion it can lead to a greater depth of awareness.

BROWN in the ORANGE digestive centre indicates some kind of illness such as an ulcer or an obstruction. For some reason the stomach is withdrawing from its function of digestion. It may also be the sign of a shy person who finds it difficult to eat in company.

BROWN in the YELLOW mind centre means someone who is entering an area which he needs to investigate on his own. He cannot share his thoughts until all the possibilities have been explored. It also indicates a monastic feeling that there is no longer any need to communicate. Too much brown means the kind of melancholia and deep depression in which people want to isolate themselves completely.

BROWN in the GREEN heart centre is a bad sign with several meanings. It may simply be that a person smokes and drinks too much. But it can suggest that he has become so emotionally traumatized that he shows constant withdrawal symptoms. He will open up to people in short bursts but then withdraw into himself completely. He cannot communicate properly with anyone.

When we have had an unhappy love affair, a crack, like a cross, will appear in the heart centre. This appears to bleed as the green energy turns into its opposite colour red. (Crossed in love our heart bleeds!) The red will go into various shades of brown before changing back to green as we begin to recover.

In bereavement a huge brown area will appear. When a much-loved person goes out of our life, part of us seems to retreat with that person. When someone close to us dies, the cords which bound us do not break off. The person leaves the body but we are linked 'elsewhere'. They will pull us away from our friends and our own world into a no-man's land where we feel totally lost.

Brown in the green centre can also mean dirty blood or too much pressure on the heart. It may indicate an imminent heart attack, which can also happen through misery, pain or fear. When the area shows no green at all, only brown, it can mean cancer of the breast or some other alien body that is sucking energy into itself.

BROWN in the BLUE throat centre is the sign of an inhibited person who keeps himself to himself, possibly because he feels he has nothing interesting or exciting to say to people. It can also mean an unhealthy throat.

BROWN in the INDIGO forehead centre is often the sign of someone repressing his natural psychic gifts. It is the sign of vulnerability and sublimation; a person who for the time being wants to withdraw from the outside world.

The opposite of white light is absence of light – or black – and we are all capable of producing both black and white within us. A mixture of white (withdrawal and silence) with black (the negative aspects of withdrawal) will be felt as a greyness when a person cannot produce energies and the chakras slow down. As this becomes deeper he will actually begin to look grey in the face and in the extreme may indicate his wish to be rid of the body itself. People manifest black and grey before they die, when there is also a loss of colour in the aura. We are capable of killing ourselves from inside.

Negative moods tune us into negative colours and once we radiate these we are automatically in tune with other people on these negative vibrations. At that moment we are in tune with all the miserable people in the word; we boost their number and bring this kind of negative thought pattern into reality. Depression is drawn to us, and through our own negativity we are drawn into black moods. Even when we are no longer depressed ourselves, the depression will continue because we are picking up that of other people. The brown and grey particles of matter we attract will stick to our aura and draw people in on that level.

Conversely, if we raise our own level of awareness into a higher sphere we will draw into our aura the vibrationary rates of all people on that level. We can watch our progress by the people we begin to meet. If we then want to lift up all the miserable people we can pour energy and love into the grey or brown consciousness. Provided we do not try this too often we may help them.

If we continually moan about meeting dull, uninteresting and unimaginative people, it should be remembered that it is we who are attracting these people to us. If, suddenly, our friends are intelligent, intuitive and helpful it is we who are now attracting them. Once we can maintain these higher vibrations and part of us is functioning on that level, we can then afford one or two unhappy moods.

With everything in life over-indulgence will produce negativity, and overcharging the centres will produce negative energies. When a centre disintegrates it pollutes all the colours in that centre. The negativity may produce a wishy-washy look as the colours lose strength and vitality, or as matters become progressively worse, it will produce grey or brown or black. At the basic level nothing is destroyed however. Even negative energies are only superimposed onto our true natural positive colours. They mix with them but do not destroy them and provided they have not gone too far, negative colours can be released to leave the true, beautiful you beneath them.

Negativity in the red reproductive centre: Over-indulgence of sex and even violent temper will set the base chakra into high speed motion and the area will begin to overcharge. Here it will turn metallic red. But far worse are those people who create fire in the basement through pornography and violent sex. Here the energy turns sour and black to the point where it may crack and cause murder and cruelty.

Ironically, when someone finds himself in this position, part of him wants to balance out and he will probably be attracted to sex with children; someone beautiful, young and attractive with the right energy. Of course this need for balance will register on another level and he does not know why he is doing it, so when he's repelled he will attack. Through his need for compensation his anger erupts. Such people can only save themselves from this horror by purifying the energy through active thought, meditation, relaxation and exercise.

There are various ways, external and internal, to boost the lower centres. But to keep exciting these energies without deep pink, spiritual love – perhaps by reaching peaks of sexual excitement with different partners – is to boost the area for the wrong reasons.

By sending beautiful colours into the universe we produce a rainbow of love. But to raise those energies on the wrong deep red and black colours (as black magic does) is to be hooked on the wrong kind of pleasure. Such activity will produce a different type of consciousness which may give insights but at the same time the chakras will disintegrate. By raising energies through the chakras by this kind of excitement, you open a dormant part of the brain to have the sensation of travelling through space or be aware of past or future lives, but you will also destroy the vehicle. The chakras will blacken at the centre; the head chakra will become dirty; the forehead will begin to crack; the heart centre will go metallic – with the risk of heart attack and the digestion will deteriorate.

Once these centres begin to fade they will need stronger boosting, and if this boost must come from inflicting pain, then the pain must become more painful and this could lead to murder. The kidneys and other organs which clear some of the redness at first will begin to collapse and once the body stops functioning properly, you must begin to pay for your fun. If not in this life, then the next.

Negativity in the orange digestive centre: If the areas below or above the orange are overcharged in any way then this centre too will overcharge. Food will be digested too quickly and not be assimilated properly. Someone who lives on his nerves rather than his body energies is overcharging on the orange centre. He will have a forced quickness about everything he does but for most of the time he will be unaware of this because he will go on and on without stopping.

It is possible, too, to over-exercise this area into too much activity and once overcharging begins the stomach will seem to switch on and off. This will produce excessive perspiration and times when we feel hot or cold for no apparent reason. Over-eating or emotional dependence on food will also produce these symptoms.

Once the area has turned metallic, a sore, irritable redness comes in and gradually black will appear. There will be increasing peristalsis and possibly ulcers. The gastric juices will stop working on the particular area they are meant to affect and move to another area; there will be a kind of cross-functioning producing belching, wind and over-acidity. Bacteria in the abdomen will multiply and there will be equal discomfort in eating or not eating. At worst it could cause cancer.

Trouble in the orange centre may first stem from problems in the base chakra. Need for energy in that area might be expressed in taking greater interest in eating and cooking. When both areas are depleted this can lead to hypochondria because to compensate for what we are lacking we become too self-oriented. We waste time thinking about different food and nutrition, doctors and cures, when it would be better to look impartially at what the problem really is.

Negativity in the yellow mind centre: Although not usually to excess, the yellow centre is the most prone to overcharging. We are never free of thoughts and we can blow up any situation by repetition. Overcharging occurs when we cannot still the mind sufficiently to find the empty spaces between our thoughts.

The stronger the mind the more destructive it can be if it hasn't learned calmness, and the more easily overcharged. But since the yellow centre in most people is not so clear and bright, there is little danger. A whirling mind usually means simply a heightened alertness as the energy moves more quickly.

The ancients wanted wisdom and aimed to produce gold in the whole of the yellow sun disc area. Energising the yellow centre will, to a certain extent, produce the wiser aspects of gold and these insights, achieved by the power of the will, can be used with the forehead energy to push us forward on our particular path. But if energising this area, we must stop before it shows red.

There is negativity not only when the centre is overcharged but also when the yellow is stagnant. People showing a good, bright yellow have clear open minds, they trust people. But a darker centre shows a mind with hidden secrets. Mustard indicates the duality in which a person may say one thing but think something completely different.

The more morbid and sickly the yellow the more undesirable the thought patterns and this negativity will undoubtedly rebound at some time in life. It will also attract people of similar thought patterns. Criminals, for example, attract other criminals to them, and if only these people were to think seriously about cleaning up their colours they would no longer be in prison because circumstances would throw them out. This may explain police corruption. A policeman needs to be very strong to avoid the danger of vibrating with criminal colours.

Illness is manifest in the emotions as well as the physical body. When black appears in the centre the negativity may cause deep depression. A schizophrenic shows yellow, red and black in this centre, but before this happens it will be a pure yellow, the sign of horrific impartiality. It means total egocentricity with no feelings at all. In this state no-one can get through to them.

Negativity in the green heart centre: Anyone involved in a sitting-down job where only the top of the body is used, is prone to negativity in the heart centre. With the pressure of responsibility, complaints, letters and business manipulation, the body constantly releases adrenalin and because of immobility the heart is continually under pressure (helped by overweight from too many business lunches). The heart is often the only place where the negativity can manifest and if the yellow mind centre below it is spinning too fast, then both will overcharge.

Through further misuse, by smoking and drinking (alcohol or coffee), plus emotional pressures and poor circulation through sitting, which is bad in itself because it is difficult to deal with anger without movement, then negative accumulation begins. The heart is the most dangerous place to overcharge.

The area will turn metallic which is not a danger point in itself, except when it goes beyond this and red appears. Then, if you also have an unhappy love affair, the energies crack and a cemetery of small black crosses will appear. If the heart is also being overcharged by the mind then grey and ice blue, too, will appear and all these colours are destructive. Until the force of attack may produce a mud colour to cover the whole area.

Many heart attacks are purely emotional and if we learned to relax they would not happen at all. Some are more dangerous in that energy begins to disappear.

We weaken in body coordination and circulation and the energies seem to appear and disappear as though the body cannot make up its mind whether it wants to be here or not. We feel enormous energy at one minute and none at all at the next; we feel alternatively hot then cold. We may not be able to think clearly at times and have pains in the upper part of the body. These are signs that the body is forcing us to rest and relax.

Negativity in the blue throat area: This happens when the thyroid is working inadequately and the glands are out of balance. Or when a singer, for example, is using his voice too much. It occurs too when we misuse the neck by swinging it every time we sit down. Negativity shows through loss of voice or the wrong colours moving into that centre. If red or black appear this indicates throat troubles or colds.

The colours in this area often change according to the people in our lives. A mother with a newly born child, for example, will show a great deal of blue. No green at all in this centre means cruelty, and the fewer the colours in the area, the narrower our field of knowledge for discussion. Cream means we are able to talk on several different subjects but are not deeply involved in any of them. More definite colours indicate that we will approach areas of interest on a far deeper level.

The mouth is the area in which everything within us is made manifest. As we have said, it is the place where the body, through breath, takes in positive colours and eliminates any colours it does not want. Negative black, dark brown and grey colours are released all the time by anyone who smokes or uses any kind of drug, including coffee, and it can be useful to constantly clear the system by imagining these colours changing to pink – if necessary after each cigarette.

Children have a strange freshness which we sense around them. This is because their out-breaths are usually a pure shade of pink or sometimes blue. Sick and unhappy people show grey in that area; secretive mind-oriented people show yellow.

Negativity in the indigo forehead centre. Misuse of this psychic visionary apparatus can overcharge this area. It is a dangerous area to overcharge because it takes us into realms for which we are not ready. It can lead to visions, paranoia, persecution mania and even madness because you are tuning into moments in past lives when the events you witness actually took place. You are operating in several dimensions at once. To be over-psychic is to be out of control and once the yellow logical side of your nature is no longer functioning properly you are thrown into a world of fantasy. Our imaginative nature should open only when the logical side is able to stabilize us.

Those who heal a great deal may take other people's negativity into the forehead area and when black appears morbidity will creep in. It is easier to survive depression on the yellow part of the third eye because the mind will produce logic as an anti-depressant. But if we are depressed on the psychic level this is very destructive. We link with unstable, psychic people and use this as an escape from the world, but in fact our own world is far safer than the one to which we are escaping.

Unless this area is strong we become too vulnerable to changes in atmosphere and to other people's misery. We lose energy from the body. We may even tune into a past life in which we felt safe, when we were under the care of someone stronger. This explains why people sometimes imagine they are someone like Napoleon. They are linking into a past life during which they were under that person's shadow and, in being controlled by them, felt safe.

Extreme anger, whether sexual, mental or emotional, will produce a tension which normal vibrations cannot overcome, and once we try to reach out beyond ordinary energies we are 'cracking up'. Any negative emotions can crack the centres and these cracks look red and angry. When an energy centre cracks, the system is faced with a dilemma because this place will have to be repaired at the expense of other areas in the body and the mending can never be instantaneous.

This extreme of emotion will often produce a fear of growing through similar experience, fear of loving again. The cracking will invariably take the body to its limit of experience but this will then often lead the body to heal itself again. In this situation we often need to reach out to unknown areas of our being and sometimes through cracking up we will reach some form of inner knowing.

In some cases, however, when we do crack up completely we link up with creation itself and fall into a darkness where the only answer is to escape from this world into eternal peace. In the end we decide not to go on with what we initially came down to experience. We should try to understand that out of any momentous depression everything we need can blossom. We have the perfect opportunity to grow into someone entirely new. By going through this 'death' we can be reborn with deeper understanding and awareness. Providing we can see them as such, all negative experiences are opportunities. They are the tools which fashion consciousness; the tools with which we can create new shapes, new moulds for ourselves.

The danger of drugs: In ancient days when the centres were smaller, drugs were taken by initiates to activate the centres to see things more clearly. Today because our centres are bigger, those who take drugs produce intense sensitivity to colour vibrations and in fact ruin the centres they are trying to see. All drugs taken into the body, including medicines, will cause chemical eruptions. The body then has to cope with these intrusions. Each of us has within us a certain colour combination and an alien combination of colours (medicines too are vibrations) causes disturbance. The helpful colours are accepted and assimilated but since all drugs have a negative affect as well as positive, the body must find an outlet for the colours it doesn't want. The centres must take part in some kind of cleansing. This is easier for younger, stronger people, but even so, when these impurities are constantly put into the body the time comes when the chakras cannot cope. They will then produce negative energy fields.

Once over-polluted the chakras cannot cleanse themselves, but at the same time they will try to spin more quickly to do so and will hit against each other as they become congested. This aggravation begins to show red, like a sore on the body. And, like the physical body, the etheric body will produce a dark scab of stale energies which form a hard, black, lifeless nucleus. Once this happens the only alternative is to stop taking drugs and try to clear the whole body, or the dark energies will split. When the body can no longer cope, illness will occur. By excessive use of drugs you are slowly killing off the body.

Hallucinatory drugs affect both the intuitive and the logical sides of the brain. Drugs force the yellow centre to spin fast to produce abnormal effects. You feel impartial but in fact you are entering the totally different world of a past life. You feel you can cope with life lived on this different level of reality, but when you come down from the high, reality becomes too stark and far less exciting. You take more to feel more interesting.

On the intuitive level you become visionary, open to mystical experience. You see, hear or feel different aspects of your being which in fact may not be the real you – nothing can be true unless it is monitored. Under the influence of drugs you cannot ask the right questions because only a strong yellow centre can do this for you. You think you are in charge and asking the right questions but all you experience is an illusion.

If the experience is beautiful you could possibly be tuning into a time when you were a mystic, but then you will realize that what you are doing is totally stupid, that there is no short cut to illumination. We walk in a world of colour. We have to learn where to look and how to look, and how to value each colour. It is a vast learning experience. There are short cuts, but like a well, you don't have to jump down to prove that there is water there. It is better to view it from above and try to learn about its depths in safety.

We often switch into past lives. If, for example, we are coping with some administration we may tune into the top of the head to borrow from that ray if we have acquired it. While we are doing so we instinctively touch those lives in which we picked up that particular colour. This is why it is dangerous to dabble – we may touch upon some horrific lives. People who have committed crimes, for instance, say they have been possessed. There *is* such a thing as 'possession' but more dangerous is to be possessed by a *part* of our being which has taken itself out of context and dropped into the characteristics of a

particular period of the past. Tremendous learning potential lies in our
memory bank, but also the potential for danger. We have a key,
provided it happens naturally and slowly. In opening into that other
mind we enter a realm in which everything is accessible, but to enter a
realm in which everything is accessible, but to enter it we have to be
superbly disciplined. Only when we learn to open this storehouse
without indulging do we avoid the dangers.

Whether you are tuning into a good or bad past life, through drugs,
the body cannot take the strain in any life, and the centres will show
red, then black and crack. If you lose your mind the forehead takes
many years to mend. Energies in that area wither and a symbolic
skeleton appears and if the other centres crack too there will be
irreversible disintegration.

White: Towards the Light

Nature will always want to help in the most suitable way, and when a
child is born he has all the colours he needs. Nature gives him balance.
But from the moment of birth he must maintain this balance through
the energies of his parents; he can draw from them the energies he
hasn't yet been able to produce. While the mother, as we have said,
radiates blue, the father usually shows red, the sexual colour, indicating
his deep need to reproduce. It takes a great deal of red energy to
consumate this need and accept the responsibility of a family. This red
with the mother's blue, produces the spiritual violet colour. When the
child has both qualities – coolness and fire – he survives well. If he
finds his supplies are not replenished and he cannot find balance this
way, he will look to other people to balance him out.

It is within our young lives that the most important changes take
place and on the whole a child can borrow colours from his brothers
and sisters, or from friends at school. But it is worth pointing out that a
quiet, sensitive child may try to supply his own needs on a psychic
level with his own imagination and be forced to live in a fantasy
world. If his parents' marriage breaks down or the family is out of
harmony through conflicting energy patterns, a child may not balance
out at all well.

We strive towards balance, to be whole and strong. But most of us
when we cannot find a colour characteristic within ourselves, will turn
to a partner for the things we lack. In other words, relationships for
most of us are based on the colour combination we need to make us
more whole. We attract what we need.

It is useful to note here that we are linked to people by 'cords'.
Imagine a human being like a sea anemone with cords that move and

pulsate from him. At the beginning of life the cords are threadlike and dormant and as the time approaches for us to meet a particular person, the cords start to thicken and pulsate.

We are corded to people through different lives or because we are due to help them in this life. All chance meetings are pre-ordained 'coincidences', although someone with a strong mind is able to change all patterns, and in this case, although certain things *should* happen they can be changed. A new future is provided.

We are all part of one another and therefore vulnerable. When a set of cords is ripped away, our hurt is felt by the earth and the universe. Something must replace them. The cords between people are very important. To make a good marriage a couple should be joined on all cords and on all centres. When the marriage fails the cording between the centres is impaired. Some cordings switch on and off, and there is great variety in thickness.

With great closeness the cords open up and form an egg shape. This egg is full of whirling energies produced by the two people. From these whirling energies an etheric seed begins to shape in the centre, and providing nothing destroys this, a child begins to shape itself. When this happens any ensuing pregnancy becomes something much deeper. The child already has a relationship with ether and this subtle relationship can be useful later.

As a general rule, if we tend towards being blue, for example, and our red centre is in bad condition we will look for someone with warmth, love and virility. Of course we must find someone who is compatible whatever our vibration, and we may find that our partner is superficially very similar to us (paradoxically like attracts like!), but it is our deep inner self that needs its complement, and it is the deeper self that matters.

Most of us are out of balance in some way and need someone to 'lean' on. If one centre is over-energized and another depleted, we will look for a partner who will replenish us. An academic man who has been using his sexual energy for the brain, for example, may fall for a woman who is less bright but very sexy. She does not need intelligence but perhaps to make him laugh. They can use each other's energies. If two people who have a good relationship are equally intellectual, the real healing process may be occurring because one partner has been hurt and needs the other, who has more deep blue in the forehead, to show kindness and consideration, or to radiate the heart energy on the green ray. This is completion, something we are all aiming for.

But things can change. Take, for example, a sensitive, artistic, violet ray girl who has too little healing ability because the forehead centre is weak. She can talk well on various subjects because she has a well-functioning throat centre but has brown in her heart centre where she has been badly hurt. She has a good brain on the yellow centre and perhaps some green in the stomach and reproductive areas which make her sensitive to the kind of men she meets.

She meets a man who is not artistic but who is aware that he wants to understand more about art and colour and painting. Here is a girl who can stimulate his interest in these things. He has a lot of natural healing in the deep blue area and this will instinctively make her feel secure. He will be faithful and attentive, which will give her healing in the forehead where she needs it most. If his throat centre is dull, which shows he does not express things well, he will find fascinating her ability with language. He will want to listen to her and she perhaps can open out his throat centre to talk more. His heart area, in good condition because an earlier affair was not very deep, can give her the green which she also needs.

In making love their energies will blend. Sex will be a comforting experience and she will feel secure and loved. She will brighten his throat centre and he her forehead and green centres. If he too is well educated the two yellow centres can be boosted because there is no depletion. Through being hurt in the past her base centre will probably be overlaid with brown but she can take some of his bright red energies. For her the whole relationship will be a healing one, but both will gain from each other.

Sexual relationships, incidentally, depend on the colour combination of the two people concerned. As different colours rise up the spine, so we have totally different sexual experiences with different people. It depends on the blend of the colours between you. No one is the same. You may produce a complete rainbow spectrum of colours together, but the quality of your climax will depend on the colours in each of your centres. The whole experience depends on your own particular vibrations and your ability to raise them to the brain. Those with open centres will experience a more spiritual type of climax; a higher form of experience altogether.

So, our couple decide to live together and the girl's energies grow stronger. Her broken heart centre will begin to mend, so too will the forehead and base centres. Gradually she will notice that she is not getting what she wants in conversation, that she needs more substance. And although she has been able to bring out some of her partner's artistic abilities, she now wants someone to teach her further. Now she is strong and does not need healing or someone else to lean on, she may meet someone with the artistic gifts she craves. And now her forehead centre is producing the kind of energies her original partner gave her, she feels the need to heal someone else. The girl who needed protection and security no longer exists.

Attraction is based on our momentary needs. We may like someone very much because he is talented musically and paints beautifully, but at the same time we actually fall deeply in love with someone who has no talent at all or who is hopeless at sex and wonder what on earth is happening. He isn't our type, we don't like what he does and cannot stand his friends. Yet there is a definite attraction and we are in fact sending out signals about what our totality should be.

Our partners (and anyone we enjoy being with) give us the colours we need, and if the energy comes into our life very strongly, infiltrating our centres, we think it must be love. We sense this rainbow of energy moving things within us and it can reach the level at which that other person is developed.

One warning. Sometimes when two people come together, one partner's colours will overshadow those of the other and the weaker in the relationship may begin to lose his identity. Obsession and total infatuation occur when one partner actually becomes the other. To tune into someone else to raise your vibratory rate is good, but if you lose your own individuality you end up as an extension of another human being, his shadow. In such circumstances, when one partner dies or there is any form of separation, the other cannot take back responsibility for themselves. They will continue to react as if the other person is still there.

If we constantly lose energy the need to be replenished can continue throughout our lives. We live our relationships within such projections and are happy to do so. But this explains why we so often realise after a certain length of time that our partner is wrong for us after all; why the attraction begins to pall. At first we sense that this person can provide missing vibrations, but once we have energized these colours, either through our partner or by ourselves, we take back responsibility for these vibrations and the attraction will obviously diminish.

We cannot spend our entire lives compensating for our faults. It should be our aim to take responsibility for our own balancing, and to find within ourselves the pot of gold at the end of the rainbow. As we balance our towards white light, we are raising ourselves on to a higher vibratory rate on which we can continue our journey. And if we reach the point of balance where the centres are energized and beginning to open and are working with different awareness, we begin to realize that we are looking for something quite different in a relationship.

We now need a more spiritual partnership, and at this point we even begin to know in the deepest aspect of our being who that person is. In the depth of our being we know there is someone with whom we are totally compatible; there is someone in the world we will recognize. A person whose vibratory rates will encompass the relationship we are seeking. There is a complementary vibratory rate for each of us, although we are not always ready for it.

We compromise in relationships because we usually do not realize that someone special exists for us and for most people this is right. That special person may not even be on earth. Sometimes the perfect person comes into your life too soon before either of you are sufficiently balanced. In this case you must reject each other until a later life. But if you are both balancing out in this lifetime, you will be drawn at first to new people with his or her qualities, until eventually the threads of the past and the cords which bind you together come into operation. The energies will grow progressively stronger until you can both come together.

Once you are complete in yourself, you and your partner will stand apart like two pillars but capable of producing a binding strength on which your dual structure can operate. Neither of you needs anything from the other in the old way because neither lacks anything. It is more a matter of adding to your partner's somethingness. You add to each other's completeness to relate on an entirely different level.

Within the meeting of two such people the love is based not on pure sexual energy but the energy of white light. You are corded an open chakras and the communication happens outside you. You relate on an energy beyond you. Sex is a melting experience, a sense of returning to the place you came from, of coming home. To reach out for gold is to be a more universal lover. When red no longer rules you can live within the spirit of rose pink. It is a higher, more ethereal experience of love and a higher level of sex. A golden person has many golden moment.

Telepathy holds the relationship together; to think of your partner is to communicate with him. Your link to past lives is closer. Energies are not wasted and there is greater opportunity to learn within the relationship, but the first priority is to work together for humanity.

Two rainbows together can go *beyond* white light.

CHAPTER FOUR

OPENING TO HIGHER CONSCIOUSNESS

So our journey in life is a means of dying to be reborn without being corded in the old sense to anyone. A path towards becoming our own white light – in varying degrees of radiance – and a state in which the coarser third eye with its seven veils of perception gives way to greater translucence.

We aim for white light not simply for ourselves but in order to affect everything else we touch. In maintaining our own balance we help to balance others (which is why the bones and garments of saints were kept sacred. Radiations are never lost – we even radiate from the grave!). Clean chakras hold light that streams through the body. If our centres are impure then we hold no reservoir of energy. Those radiating in white light breathe out pure or golden white, the colour of silence.

But how can we truly achieve white light when so many colours invade our centres? Can we ever be a clear channel? At lease we can try. We should begin by taking time to sit quietly; we should try to live, as the holy men did, in calmness and dignity. And like these who refused help, we should aim to find our true selves on our own.

As man's knowledge and ability to see the invisible diminished, he became more conscious of the colours around him. So in our search for colour consciousness let's begin with that. Begin by examining a typical week in your life. Look at what you enjoy and what sort of time you give to any one activity.

In which chakras are you orientated? Do you recognize an imbalance? At the same time, look at the colours around you. Although we may not consciously know that we are walking around in a coloured bubble, a clue may be there. Why are we drawn to, say, yellow wallpaper or a yellow coat? Are we *externalizing* our inner radiations?

We can see that the colours we choose to wear or to live with are a reflection of a momentary or long-term state of our being. If we are aware that colour matters, that it is something we are acting within, we may slowly begin to notice some secrets about ourselves.

We are all deeply affected by the clothes we wear. A fashion model is changed by wearing a different outfit or a different colour. Fashion is often originated by people oriented on the violet ray who tune into a need for certain colours ar a certain time. Indeed, fashion in terms of colour can be used for personal or cultural change. Remember, too, that what we wear, others must look at. Our choice will affect everyone else around us.

Of course there are many hues and tones of colour and we need the artist's expertise to understand the infinite variety. But instinct plays a large part in our choice. We wear a colour and know instinctively whether it looks wrong. A year later this same colour may look right, which indicates that changes have occurred in our chakras. Remember, however, that a colour may repel us because we have a need for this particular vibration. We should try to sense when we are rejecting a colour for the wrong reasons; when to wear a colour to suit or contrast our mood.

We are looking here at disharmony in our bodies through wrong colour vibrations. In the first instance we can deal with them in a practical way. By looking at what we wear, the colours of the foods we eat, at our surroundings. We can begin to analyse how much these colours are part of our idea of life:

RED, as we have said, is associated with the reproductive area and should only be worn after careful thought. Red is a violent colour; certainly red walls should be avoided. Red, however, is helpful for those undersexed and for women who cannot conceive. A red lamp in the bedroom will help this colour to be absorbed.

ORANGE tips the flames in the fire, and orange can fire and inspire us. It is an active, invigorating colour with neither the intellect of yellow nor the sexuality of red. Those feeling depressed or lethargic should wear this bright, warm, friendly colour. Orange, linked with nature and the seasons helps digestion, but too much orange may make you eat more. Bright orange brings a wideawake feeling; you'll get up more easily in the morning.

PEACH is orange on a higher vibration. For some it is the colour of spiritual love and relates to a more advanced person who has made interesting journeys on the soul level. It may look wrong on some people. A good strong peach however, is helpful in a bedroom. It has a wonderful effect on the skin and keeps us youthful. Insipid peach, however, will provoke lethargy since the energies are encouraged to move to a different level. Delicate pink shades have the same effect.

YELLOW: the practical colour and linked to the left side of the brain, will help those who find it difficult to study; those too impractical, too artistic or too open. If the intellectual side of your life is overactive, reduce this colour.

GREEN is the colour of balance; between practical yellow and healing blue. Green is beneficial to the nervous ystem. It combats high blood-pressure, it is helpful for a strained heart. Green is calming, but with so much green in nature, those with sluggish chakras at the surface of the skin will become lethargic with too much green. Living in a concrete jungle without parks or gardens can unbalance the system; green should play an important role in choice or clothes and decor.

BLUE is a healing, calming colour. If you live with an aggressive who at times has red in his aura, wearing blue will calm them down. Pale blue is good for the eyes. Living in a climate where skies are always grey, blue — the colour that links us with the sky and sea — should be worn.

If you have to give a lecture, wearing turquoise, the colour of communication, will help your self expression. Turquoise is good to bring shy or quiet people out into the world. Blue is also good for babies, since the mother's aura shows blue during pregnancy.

DARK BLUE colours, the higher healing colours, do not suit everyone. Wearing this colour you may tune too much into the third eye which is not beneficial. Only ever pain one wall in a room dark blue. Men who wear dark blue suits may have an unconsicous desire to heal.

Those sensitive to VIOLET, the colour said to being 'death to this life', may find themselves sensing other dimensions; aware of work done out of the body. It will certainly be difficult to get up in the morning!

In ancient days MAGENTA, the mix of the three prime colours, was considered to be important — along with purple. It is the colour or organization and an office painted magenta should improve this quality plus your general awareness and ability to cope with life.

In considering colour, the stronger more decisive it is, the greater the effect. 'Wishy-washy' colours will be less effective. The closer to the body, too, the more concentrated the effect. The mix too is important. Red alone is an aggressive colour; blue is calming. Together they form purple, a neutral colour which is neither hot nor cold. They lost their identity in the mix. Examine the mix at any one time in your wardrobe. By wearing a yellow blouse with a grey skirt or putting layers of colour one on top of the other, the effects are combined. Natural fibres, incidentally, are better than synthetic.

Colour is vibration and the mixtures created produce sounds on our bodies. Just as certain notes played together on the piano sound off-key, so certain shades together produce discord. When we notice how wrong an outfit looks, it may be that our aura is out of harmony. We may need more simple clothes. Incidentally, sound – which is colour itensified – is even more potent than colour and in the future it will be used as a way of cleansing, healing and purifying the etheric body.

On the whole we dress for our own well-being. We surround ourselves with the colours we need, especially if we live alone. Living with a partner, however, may change things. The moods of that partner may be taken into consideration. Their colours should complement ours. If our partner wears bright colours and the decor is bright, we may be absorbing enough brightness. We ourselves may not need to dress brightly. Remember, too, that a passionate involvement in clothes may indicate our need to compensate for what a partner cannot give.

Weather affects the clothes we choose. The chakras react to sunshine and bright blue sky. As grey in the aura is a sign of illness and the slowing down of the chakras, so grey skies, grey pavements and grey houses, slow down our chakras until they are so lazy they hardly move at all.

People who wear grey are often those who make judgements. A man who wears a grey suit may be a good critic. Those who lack judgement should wear grey, but often dark grey, such a practical colour, is used in school uniform and it's no wonder that children criticise their teacher, their school, their parents. Drabness slows people down. Our surroundings can be grim; office, school, classroom can adversely affect us, and more imagination could be used in terms of colour.

We are also assailed by propaganda. Clever minds package goods to make them more attractive. Food, often coloured to make it more appealing, can affect us. If you are attracted by a product ask yourself why those colours are drawing you. When a shop window or a poster catches your eye, ask what the colour means to you. Producers are clever at promoting colour vibrations we don't need. Blue and other refreshing colours, for example, are sometimes used in advertising to counteract something harmful.

The ancients painted frescoes on their walls or in their caves. They put up tapestries to represent the outer world. Scenes of dolphins, grouse, the natural world were used and by imagining nature they actually absorbed her. The imagination is a powerful too. Wallpaper, too, has a powerful effect. A red wallpaper will be aggressive; a geometric design will affect the solar plexus. Wallpaper with orange or a kitchen design will affect the digestive centre. A wall full of food won't help the compulsive eater. A paper of flowers will lead to the heart centre. One that takes you into open spaces will affect the higher centres. We are also affected by the vibrations of the designer.

We may be drawn to a wallpaper through the influence of past lives. Look at the colours it contains and sense others that are missing. See if the design reminds you of a particular period in history, and sense perhaps which period you are linked to. Certain colours can link you into a past life and change your personality.

The colours we choose may reflect the mood we are moving into or conversely what we need to compensate. According to our needs we will attract different vibratory rates to us. Gradually we can begin to know whether we like these colours because we *are* those colours or whether we are drawn to them at this moment because we *need* them.

Some people may need sickly yellow and brown colours, for example. They need to externalize the secret side of their being. At this moment they are too scared to look out on the world. Brown, the monastic colour is the colour of Mother earth. We find brown leather chairs pleasing. Brown is a protective colour and we feel protected surrounded by brown carpets, furniture or clothes. It is inadvisable, however, to have too much brown on walls. We should balance our rooms between earth and sky colours. Green, the balancer may be found in plants.

There may be certain flowers we need or certain colours within those flowers. In buying flowers for someone else, consider the colours you choose. If you are buying for yourself, sense what colour you would like around you. Choosing white or red flowqers may be less automatic than you think. Once you have chosen the decor of your house you are stuck with it. Flowers may be the only change to be made, the only accessory that allows you to tune into your chaning moods.

WHITE is an interesting colour. As we have said, we are on a journey towards 'white light'. While some peole live happily with white walls, others find it more difficult. Those more purified people who experience instant karma, may be upset by specks of dirt on this whiteness. And those less purified may also have a problem with white walls. If a centre is tinged with black, white light in a room will motivate the body to cleanse itself. Turning into the whiteness may cause a violent reaction. As the etheric releases into the body, there may be symptoms such as a temperature, a cold or gastric trouble.

CREAM, a neutral colour, is the colour of variety. A cream person is one who is interested in a wide variety of things – he goes with everything. A room with cream walls can have accessories in almost any other colour.

SILVER, too, is a useful colour. Adaptable 'quick-silver' people can do many things and many colours tone with silver, as those who collect silver objects know. It's a colour to combat lethargy.

GOLD never adversely affects us. Our journey in life is to open to the golden qualities within us. Touches of gold in a room are important.

Walls, gloves handbags, underclothes, socks, hats, all affect us. For some people this effect can be quite dramatic. For others more closed – yellow intellectual people perhaps – nothing will affect them deeply. It depends on our attentiveness to colour. When we first change the colouring of a room it will affect us more deeply because we are more conscious of the change. When we become acclimatized to certain colours around us, our system closes off. Again, some people close off better than others.

Basic laws of colour prevail, but of course two different people wearing exactly the same colour will give it their own special qualities. Everyone is different. According to the amount of a colour we have at the top of the head – the record of our spiritual progress – we will tune into that colour more or less. However, we all have our own survival kit which prevents us tuning in too drastically. We may be tuning into a higher level but not consciously receiving it through the body.

From the moment we wake in the morning we can *sense* the colour we are in. When we feel blue or grey with depression, for example, our nature is too cool and heavy and we affect everyone else in this way. We paint the picture of what we are at any one moment. We colour our lives. We change them. We are our own best artists. The body is our palette and we choose our own mix of colours. We have an automatic colour system, but just as our digestion malfunctions if we eat the wrong food, so our colour system goes wrong if we surround ourselves with the wrong colours.

But as we have seen, colour is not simply on the outside. We must regain our ability to 'see' those on the inside; move a little closer towards an inner awareness; or, in other words, towards healing ourselves through colour. This sounds a far harder task but there is in fact profound simplicity in healing. All it needs is a willingness to empty the cup before it is refilled; to lose the attitudes which prevent us healing ourselves. Above all, it needs TRUST.

We have spoken already about *breathing*, relaxation and *meditation*.

These are the tools that link our etheric and physical bodies and ultimately connect us to the other vehicles which make up our wholeness; the harmony within ourselves.

Tuning in is the important factor. We constantly deal with the invisible world, but we each use different equipment to sense it; one person, the clairvoyant, may *see* what is going on. Another – perhaps the majority of us – may *sense* things. By turning our attention to the importance of colour we will immediately be in touch with it. We must practise a little each day.

To tune into the invisible world of colour we must begin by thinking of the protective vehicle around us; the aura.

Lying down, breathe up the back of your body and down the front. Sense the aura placing your mind on worlds around it. Do this seven times, each time moving your mind further away from the head, feet and body. Now breathe up the right side of your body and down the left – again seven times – enlarging the aura until you have created a large sensory space: an egg shape. By doing this you are tuning into higher bodies and into the top of your head – and colour.

Relaxation is a release mechanism. Before you can go consciously into the body you must be deeply relaxed; not asleep but aware. Begin by tensing the feet, then relax and feel the feet open a little. Tighten the knees, relax them and open. Continue up the body, through the lower abdomen, the hips, the heart area, shoulders, elbows, hands and throat. Then allow the whole surface of the skin to feel relaxed and open. The forehead will automatically open further as it is relaxed and you contact the top of the head awareness.

As you lie still and peaceful, your brainwaves should have changed a little and you should feel more creative. For any kind of colour meditation you must relax as many centres as possible. Imagine the atmosphere changing; that the whole surface of your skin has changed. This awareness will affect other chakras. Imagine what it would be like if everything was relaxed. Feel that you do not exist; that the room is there but you can walk through walls. In other words, try to feel empty.

How do you choose colours? What shade of red for the basement? What kind of blue for the forehead? How does your conscious knowledge of colour compare to the body colours?

One way is to eliminate the problem simply by drawing white light through the body, allowing each part to absorb what it needs. Breathe deeply allowing the outbreath to eliminate negativity.

Or you can be more positive and draw particular colour vibrations into the centres. In doing this it is better to link yourself with whatever that colour represents, to sense the vibratory feeling rather than the colour itself. To bring deep blue into the forehead, for example, try to think of the moments in which you felt protection, a sense of absorbing goodness.

To replenish the throat area, first stop talking. Even when it is still, the tongue may be in an active place. Move it further up or down to put out of action. The throat is our centre of communication. Tune into the qualities of a good communicator, someone with this unemotional, cool, restful colour. Feel the colour spread you out, as the sky and sea spread. Let the throat open.

To draw colour into the heart area, think of Nature. She has a wide variety of greens, but by tuning into the healing properties of plants and trees this area will automatically regenerate. Feel totally at peace, empty of your past emotions.

To draw yellow into the mind area imagine a quiet, silent place like a library. Feel your energy becoming receptive to its knowledge.

The sense of orange is being comfortable, content and full, of having eaten the right things. Red is the warmth of being cared for and loved.

Jewels, which are condensed energy, also provide us with colour vibrations. They may help you assess the rightness of colour. Stones can help arthritis or cure headaches, and they heal generally. If we are drawn to or have an affinity with a particular jewel, it is because we need its protection. Once we can tune into a stone in our imagination we no longer need that jewel.

In this kind of consciousness we can also feel our way into colour through meditation. Imagine a beautiful evening sky with orange-red colours to be absorbed into the base centres. Meditate on walking through Nature, designing your own path through to the area in the heart. Think of seas and skies and imagine them in your throat area. Imagine yourself in the deeper colours of the night, resting in your forehead. To imagine white, think of crisp, deep snow. To feel pure light, sense the radiations coming through and think of the spectrum unified into one.

For some this is difficult. If your imagination is poor it is better to look at a jewel or something more tangible, then close the eyes and feel the colour.

Through meditation we can begin to purify ourselves until we reach the state of mind in which we cannot destroy. Ultimately we may reach the point at which simply to be is a state of meditation. And as our breath and meditations clear out the toxins from our etheric circulation, *exercise* can begin to rid the body of this pollution (see end of chapter). We must learn to be in constant movement towards white light. Each step is a step in consciousness.

We must try to release our relationship to colour vibrations. We must reach the point where we can sense or touch two colours with our eyes closed and feel the difference. We can try to feel that some colours are heavy, some lighter. We can also try to sense colour with other parts of the body; from the back of the body instead of the front; or sitting on a certain colour. Our sensing equipment is very little used. We should be able to walk barefoot on various colours and feel them through the feet.

A huge cosmetic industry encourages us to pain ourselves – our faces, nails, hair – every colour they can think of. We are encouraged to be colourful beings. We can paint on colour but this will not create beauty. Beauty comes from our inner colours. To stay young, to have beautiful skin texture, we must produce those colours inside; and it's cheaper.

The more aware we become of colour and nature, the more colour and nature tune into us. We can feed from colour, plants, flowers. This awareness will change our body; it will become lighter and younger. Only then can we begin to look more truly beautiful. It won't matter any more how we look on the outside because our colours will radiate from within. A bathed and painted person sometimes doesn't 'feel' right to our deeper senses. We sense when inner colours are wrong.

Opening to a true relationship to colour is really an opening to angelic realms, to God consciousness. What the Church calls 'a state of Grace' is to radiate beautiful colours; colours that have many levels, each more and more ethereal.

Relationships with others are colour relationships and the more we change, the more others will notice those changes. Nor will we ever be lonely. Once the aura is a place of beauty where other people feel at home, we become a person that everyone takes to. We are surrounded by people, even the shyest ones open up to communicate. The more aware we are of colour, the more aware we are of ourselves and the more we will change. And as we change we recognize within us the need to cure, to heal, to understand others, to be a worthwhile person in a world where so many values are being destroyed. We are now in the process of building up a new world, a new reality to take over from the old. A process by which it becomes possible to be in tune with all people and all religions; to extend our aura in total love. Total love means being so much part of the higher consciousness of colour that we are saturated with its strength. All these faculties are open to us.

Colour consciousness is a search, an adventure. It is losing ourselves to find ourselves again. It is the most beautiful thing we will ever do in our lives.

CHAPTER FIVE

ENERGIZING EXERCISES

Yoga on the physical level is to do with energizing the glands in our body, and with working on the circulation and lymphatic system. It is the process of purifying these major areas to give health to the body. But, as a further and natural extension of this it is also to open to a higher level of awareness. The ultimate is to reach out for a different, wider field of reality. The real purpose of yoga is to unfold methodically the powers which lie dormant within each of us. In its true sense yoga means 'union with all worlds'.

To begin yoga may be regarded as a therapy. A technique to promote health, to put everything in our body in its right place and in correct working order. But, by activating the glands, the lymphatic system and circulation, the chakras are automatically activated and more energy is produced in the centres.

Yoga can build up the areas in need and, in simple terms, a 'hard' person will often become softer and more understanding, while a soft and sensitive person will often find strength. In other words, by practising yoga we are strengthening colours in our chakras to promote balance and to widen our scope in any particular direction.

In the beginning it is advisable to exercise for as little as fifteen minutes. Too much initial enthusiasm may do more harm than good. Work up gradually until you sense automatically how much movement to do in any one day.

In working on the energy centres there should be a warning about holding yoga postures. Holding is good when a chakra is depleted or dirty, but to hold an exercise in an area that is overcharged may have an adverse effect. As a general rule, an exercise is perfectly effective if held for only a short time.

In the normal course of events these things cause few problems. By doing yoga once a week and none at home, you can go on for years without awareness of such things. A few exercises and some relaxation will simply improve your health and sociability, to the extent that you feel more relaxed. But taken more seriously, over a period of time you will begin to sense something changing within you. Your consciousness will begin to shift. This is the time when expert guidance is needed and why one expert has said he would not allow someone to teach yoga before at least ten years training.

There is, incidentally, no point in trying to boost a centre through exercise without concentrating on the area it is meant for. Nor in working on a position for fun, without thinking of its higher purpose. Once all the centres are open, energies will automatically travel in and out and there is less need to worry about these things, but since few of us have open centres, we should attempt to take ourselves seriously. Once the centres are open the exercises may also be done in any order. Since the energies are then coming in from the top of the head, there is no need to work from the base of the body upwards.

Eventually we can begin to know which exercises we need to boost a depleted chakra and which we need to avoid in order not to exacerbate an already over-charged energy centre. Quite simply, if we lack vitality then we know the stomach energy is depleted. If we don't want sex, the base energy is depleted.

Centres have inevitably become refined as we have evolved from primitive man towards sophistication. As a result modern man has far larger chakras than the ancients; his centres interweave much more closely. Consequently, any exercise aimed to energize one particular centre will automatically energise others, particularly those above or below. The effectiveness also depends on how often the exercise is done and how long it is held for each time.

We obviously cannot give colours for all the exercises in existence, but in the following section we will give in sequence a selection of exercises that charge the major seven centres of the body. In each group we will work from the simplest movements towards the more difficult. These exercises are a first stage towards working on our centres.

You may take the whole sequence of seven and use this as a typical weekly yoga class. Or incorporate one exercise from each section into a shorter perhaps daily routine. Obviously the more you do the greater the benefit.

When yoga arrived in the West it was linked with physical training to make it more acceptable to Western ideas. Teachers chose to use standing exercises and many classes still concentrate on these. But it is often better to work from the horizontal position. Those whose posture is bad (and you can check for a hollow back by standing against a wall), and those with varicose veins, should definitely avoid standing classes. Standing in one place can be unhealthy, even if the feet are apart (this can throw the body forward) and most of us who have not exercised at all should concentrate on exercises performed sitting or lying down.

We have much to learn about the body and although sitting down does give slight pressure on the spine, at least the body can move forward more cautiously. By beginning many of the exercises lying on a flat hard surface, the shoulder blades are forced inwards. The shoulders and spine can come down slightly and breathing slowly in and out of this position gives a better overall posture. As Mathias Alexander, who introduced a technique of psycho-physical balance, said, most of us accumulate a lifetime of bad habits in merely sitting down. To rid ourselves of this we need lots of exercise from the floor.

Avoid a yoga class with too many students, in which a teacher cannot possibly meet everyone's needs or register their changes. Good teachers do not advertise, they are found, so shop around. Try a class before joining it and sense what is happening. Does it make you too sexy, or hyper-active afterwards? Are the students friendly? Who works on their exercises at home? Hatha yoga is the best discipline to begin. It is the branch of yoga philosophy which deals with the physical body, its health, well-being and strength.

Once the muscles are strong and supple any movement will ripple through the entire body and the fitter you become the less exercise you will need.

We are what we eat. Try to eat more wholesome food. Avoid tinned foods. Eat a wide variety of fruit and vegetables but less cakes, coffee and chocolate. Drink plenty of water and juices. If you have dirty blood, exercise simply moves the stagnating toxins around the body. But do not give up meat unless you sense that your whole system is changing. Eventually, as you begin to clean up, you may find meat less easily digested and a preference for vegetables.

Do not eat for at least two hours before exercise.

Never exercise after a long period of sunbathing.

Breathing should be through the nose. To clear the right nostril, place the right hand in the left armpit and press the elbow on the left towards the body. Repeat on the other side.

Exercise on a mat to support the body.

Wear comfortable, loose-fitting clothing; preferably a leotard or exercise tights and shirt.

Remove neck jewellery, spectacles and wrist watches.

Relax before and after an exercise but as a relaxation before continuing on to the next movement.

Come out of a pose immediately you feel any discomfort; remember it isn't a competition.

The ancients were naturally supple. We are not. Our comfortable way of life precludes that. Chairs, as a simple example, have twisted our hips out of their natural shape. Therefore, no exercise should be attempted without first loosening up. Before each session, lie flat on the back and stretch. Then systematically contract and relax the muscles in the body from toe to top, including the arms and hands. Finally, sit up and make small movements with the legs to loosen them.

Make no effort at all the first time you move into a position. On the second attempt let go a little more. The third time you can make a little more effort.

As a general rule, do not try any pose more than three times, but gradually you will sense for yourself how much you need to do.

If you sense that one or two centres are depleted more than others, use a short daily routine using exercises from these groups. But, more important, if you sense that one particular centre is overcharged, leave out the exercises from this group altogether.

Remember that for the desired effect you must *concentrate* on the area you are working on during that exercise.

Energizing the Red Centre

1. Lie flat on the back and raise one leg up in the air. Bend it at the knee and bring the knee to the chest, keeping the other leg flat on the floor. If necessary, hold the knee with both hands to bring it further into the chest. On the in-breath raise the forehead to the knee, hold for a moment and release back on the out-breath. Repeat on the other side. Then, lift both legs together on the in-breath and press the knees to the body on the out-breath.

This exercise activates the base of the spine. Raising the legs will draw the blood down relieving the veins, at the same time increasing the circulation of blood in the base of the stomach. An American orthopaedic surgeon suggests that all our problems originate from bad posture. Inability to bring the knee to the body in this simple exercise may indicate later spinal problems and other discomfort. It alleviates wind and constipation.

Once the exercise is complete, strengthen the leg and stomach muscles by sitting up without help from the hands.

2. Once sitting, bend at the knees and bring the heels into the buttocks. Lean back a little and lift the right leg until straight on the in-breath, stretching the arms towards the foot. Hold for a few moments and bring the hands and leg down on the out-breath. Repeat on the other side. Then, maintaining balance, raise both legs together as straight as possible on the in-breath. Stretch the arms out straight.* Lower on the out-breath.

This exercise stretches the hamstrings, improves balance and works on the thigh and abdominal muscles. It improves nervous tension and poor digestion.

---

* When stretching out the arms in any exercise, do so as to a child, with love and harmony, not with agression.

3. In the sitting position, cross the right leg over the left leg and bring the right foot down on the floor close to the knee. On the in-breath, run the hand over the raised knee down to hold the instep and open the leg out to the side as straight as possible. Hold for a moment and slowly bring the leg back into position on the out-breath. Do this once or twice and repeat on the other side. On the in-breath, draw both feet in, taking one instep in each hand and raise up both legs together as straight as possible, balancing on the buttocks. Come down slowly on the out-breath, bending the knees as the feet are lowered to the floor. Those more experienced may hold this position of balance and take a few breaths.

This exercise improves balance, stretches the hamstrings and works on the inner thighs.

4. Bend the right leg at the knee. Raise it and bring it back by holding the right foot with the left hand and inserting the right arm through the leg from the inside. Press the thigh back a little. While sitting in this position, take a breath and on the out-breath try to bring the foot as close to the top of the head as possible, then release. Take a second breath and on the out-breath bring it close to the forehead. On the third out-breath move it as close to the waist as possible. Then slip the foot on to the left thigh and move the knee up and down a few times. Repeat this on the other side. Never press the knee down with the hand from the top. Rather place the hand underneath and allow the knee to move the hand down.

Then, leaning back slightly for balance, lift both legs and balance on the buttocks. Place the arms on the inside of the knees and pass the hands under the knees until the legs rest comfortably in the crook of the arms. Open the arms to the sides as much as possible, stretching the thighs further apart. Hold as long as possible. Gaze at a fixed point to help maintain balance.

All these exercises work the body towards the full *Lotus*, the ideal exercise for the reproductive area.

5. Cross the feet a short distance from the body and slowly, with support of the hands, push the buttocks forward as close to the heels as possible. The various lotus positions energise the lower part of the abdomen with the feet and cuff off circulation from both sides of the body. But to begin we should attempt the *half-lotus*.

From the cross-legged position lift one foot, sole up, on to the opposite thigh. Use alternate feet each time you try so the circulation is cut off from both sides in turn.

To eventually achieve the full Lotus position, place the right foot against the left side of the groin, sole up. Bending the left leg at the knee, lift the ankle and slowly place the foot against the right side of the groin. This takes time to accomplish and no pressure should be exerted by the hands to bring the knees lower down. The hands may be placed palm up or down and the first finger touch the joint of the thumb with the rest of the fingers straight. But you will begin to sense what your hands want to do.

6. Sit in the lotus position, or simply with legs crossed. To allow the energy to move up towards the head, on the in-breath make a small stretch by running the hands slowly over the body, stretching back a little as you do so and come down slowly towards the right knee on the out-breath. Keep the back as straight as possible. Place the hands on both sides of the knee. Repeat on the other side. Then, on the in-breath, move the hands over the body once more and on the out-breath bring the head down as far as possible between the legs, supporting yourself with the hands if necessary.

Once balance is achieved in these positions, sit upright and clasp the fingers behind. On the in-breath, slowly bend the body forward, raising the arms as high behind as possible, until the forehead touches or is as near to the ground as possible. Slowly return on the out-breath.

Anyone overcharged in this area must take care to avoid exercises that bring the feet towards the groin because the energies in the feet will give extra boost. Do not press the groin or cut off the circulation in any way.

For those with a bad back, sit in a comfortable chair and lift the legs to stimulate that area.

Energizing the Orange Centre

Stretching the legs in front one at a time or both together tends to deplete the red centre a little. The energy is pushed out when we bend forward. However, in doing this, we are now energizing the stomach area.

1. In the sitting position, bend the right leg at the knee and place the foot close to the knee of the other leg. Allow the knee to drop to the side and lean slightly towards the knee with the body. Place the hands behind the back, linking the fingers behind the small of the back and slowly move the body forward a little, moving the heel as close as possible to the top of the thigh.

Bring the hands over the leg and the body on the in-breath, lean back slightly and stretch, coming down towards the knee on the out-breath. Relax gently. Place the left hand under the left ankle, or anywhere comfortable along that leg and open the opposite arm and stretch back on the in-breath. Hold for a few moments and then come down breathing out. Do this two or three times and once more do a small stretch over the body on the in-breath moving forward on the out-breath. This time try to bend a little lower, but still without strain. Repeat on the other side.

When this feels easy, repeat with the foot placed on the thigh in the half-lotus position, close to the groin, and use the same method of coming forward.

Now bring the legs together, knees slightly raised if necessary. Breathe in slowly and run the hands over the legs, bringing the elbows in slightly. Lengthen the body, stretch back and come forward on the out-breath, resting on the legs without strain. Do this several times.

When the head easily reaches the knees, try these variations:

a. Before stretching the arms over the head, clasp the hands together. As you bend slowly towards the feet, place the clasped hands over the feet and allow the body to lie along the legs. Clasping the toes, and without hunching, use the elbows to put the body down to the legs until the forehead is on the knee. The legs should remain flat on the floor.

This powerful exercise tones the abdominal organs. It benefits the bladder and prostate gland.

b. Clasp the hands behind and on the out-breath, bend forward from the hips, bringing your nose on the knees and raising the hands as far up behind as possible. Relax the back muscles and breathe slowly.

2. The following exercise energizes the yellow and red centres as well as the orange, but should be practised with concentration on the stomach area. When there is concentration there is a boost.

Move on to all-fours, like a cat, placing the hands directly in line with the knees so they are located beneath the shoulders. On the in-breath sink the spine as much as possible, at the same time raising the head. On the out-breath, lower the head, arch up the spine and clench the buttock muscles. Repeat several times.

To vary the exercise, put the chin down on to the floor between the hands on the in breath.

This exercise flexes the spine, neck and shoulders and eases menstrual problems.

3. In the same position, looking straight ahead, lift one knee on the in-breath and bring it in as close to the chest as possible. Look down at the knee and touch it with your nose. On the out-breath, stretch the leg behind. Then bend the knee and raise the leg as high as possible, stretching back the neck and looking up. Slowly return and repeat with the other leg. During this exercise, relax the body and concentrate on its flowing movement which helps the spine, the sciatic nerve and the female reproductive organs.

To vary this exercise, raise alternate hand and leg.

4. From the 'cat' position, kneel up. Stretch a little to strengthen the thighs by moving the body back and forward, either with hands on hips or outstretched.

Then sit on the heels with the knees together and bring the hands behind. Clenching the buttocks a little, rise up and lean back.

When this becomes easy, as the thighs are stronger, come slowly down on the arms and elbows until the head touches the ground and the back is fully arched. If this is comfortable, support the body weight with the hands again and lower the back of the head and neck to the floor until the shoulders are down. The knees must remain on the ground. Concentrate on the abdomen or the breath and hold for a few moments. Then, using the arms and elbows, raise the body again. Once the thighs are really strong you may raise without the arms.

In this exercise, the feet too concentrate energy on the orange area to alleviate constipation and abdominal ailments.

Energizing the Yellow Centre

The yellow centre, the one between the heart and the stomach, is one of the most misused in the body. Almost everyone slouches and the heart and mind centres are so co-ordinated that unless the spine works well, neither can function properly. Someone who holds himself straight and tall will automatically release the pressure between the mind and emotions. By bringing the whole body forward we can open up the area of the spine in which the yellow centre operates.

1. From the kneeling position, bend the body forward, push the hands out in front and have a good stretch forward. On the in-breath, bring the hands round behind, and lower the buttocks (inability to do this may mean back trouble later). On the out-breath bring the top of the head down in front of the knees. Rest a moment, then bring the hands forward and place them palms one on top of the other. Rest the forehead on top. Close the eyes and relax, resting the back of the neck.

The effect of this position works slowly and can be held for longer than most. It is good for lower back trouble and lumbago.

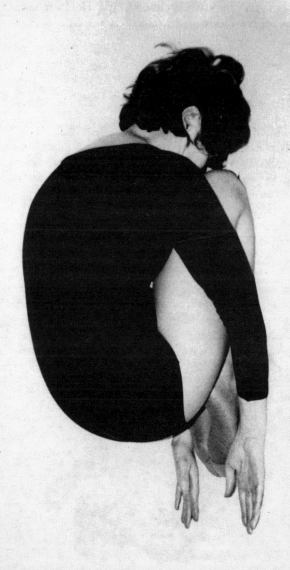

2. Sit up. Bring the feet together and the hands behind (the further the hands come behind the more difficult it is to achieve). On the in-breath, raise the buttocks and clench a little. Hold a moment and come down on the out-breath.

Once more advanced, lift one leg at a time from the raised position.

A second variation is to place one foot, then the other, on to the opposite thigh before raising the buttocks.

This exercise may be practised with feet together or slightly apart.

3. From this last position, where the legs were straight and arms behind, bend the legs at the knees and open them up. Raise the buttocks and bring the head back a little. Lower. Then repeat and keeping the knees up, lie down on the spine stretching the arms behind. Bring the heels in towards the buttocks with feet about one foot apart. Place the palms on the ground beside the head with fingers pointing towards the shoulders. Slowly push up until the weight of the upper body rests on the crown. Lower slowly until the head and neck rest on the floor. With hands under the hips walk the legs forward until the body is down.

Eventually, by adjusting the hands inwards slightly, you should aim to push up until the legs and arms straighten and the body is fully arched before lowering.

This exercise benefits the nervous and glandular systems.

4. Lie on the stomach. On the in-breath bend the knees and grasp the ankles with the hands. Tense the leg muscles and arch the back. Lift head and chest and pull the thighs up as high as possible from the floor, keeping the arms straight. Slowly return on the out-breath.

Once this pose is comfortable, rock backwards and forwards as you breathe in and out, concentrating on the abdomen or the back.

This exercise is powerful massage for the abdominal organs and muscles and the joining of the hands and feet over the yellow centre emphasizes that energy.

5. Lie flat on the floor face down, legs together, with the top of the feet resting on the floor and arms by the sides. Rest the chin on the floor. Take an in-breath and on the out-breath raise the legs from the floor as high as possible, keeping them straight. Contract the buttocks and thigh muscles trying to keep the legs together. Hold for as long as comfortable and slowly lower the legs. Relax fully.

Beginners should place clenched fists as far beneath the thighs as possible and use them to lift one leg at a time. When this becomes easy push both legs up with the hands.

This exercise is good for hips, abdomen, pelvis and lower back. We include it in this section because most people can only raise their legs half-way along the body, corresponding to the yellow centre.

Energizing the Green Centre
The most beneficial exercise for the heart area is the twist.

1. Place the right foot over the left knee and on to the ground on the outside of the left knee, holding the right knee with the right hand. Place both hands together around the knee and bring the chin down. On the in-breath lift the spine and head. On the out-breath, swing the left arm back, taking the body round as far as it will go. Hold for several moments and very slowly bring the arm back breathing in. On the out-breath bring the head down again. Do this two or three times and then repeat on the other side.

To extend this exercise, put the right hand under the right toe and stretch back once more, but do not attempt the more difficult pose if you cannot stretch the spine well.

2. Again sit with the legs straight in front. Bring the right leg across and place the foot flat on the floor outside the left knee. Place the left heel up against the right buttock. The right knee should be as near to the left armpit as possible. Bring the left arm and shoulder over the right knee and put the hand under the knee then round behind the back. Try to link hands behind. Turn the back and neck round to the right as far as is comfortable without straining. Repeat on the other side.

This exercise is excellent for the vertebrae and the spinal nerve endings.

3. Lie flat on the floor with the arms by the sides. Using the elbows for support, raise the body up arching the spine. Let the head back until the crown touches the ground. Lift the hands to the prayer position on the chest. Beginners should leave their legs flat on the ground, those more advanced can raise the legs a little. Breathe deeply and slowly holding the position for as long as possible. Lower the legs to the ground and use the elbows for support to lower the body and neck to a relaxed position.

This exercise stretches the intestines and abdominal organs, and subsidiary chakras in the elbows emphasize the energy to the heart area.

4. This may be done from the lotus position for the more advanced, or simply by crossing the legs. Using the elbows for support, bend backwards until the crown of the head touches the ground. Bringing the hands forward and grasping the big toes (if in the lotus position), or placing them on the thighs try to bring the elbows down to the ground at each side. Arch the back as much as possible, since the area raised is the area boosted.

This position stretches the intestines and other abdominal organs. It also encourages deep breathing.

5. Kneel up and on the in-breath raise the arms slowly forward and bring them up. On the out-breath bring them slowly back, bending the fingers back slightly, and arching the back as much as possible. Breathe in coming forward, letting the body drop gently forward on the out-breath.

6. Kneel with the toes on the floor and the feet and knees apart. Leaning backwards stretch the arms to the side and place the hands on to the heels. Stretch the neck backwards and arch backwards as far as possible, keeping the hips well forward. Return to the kneeling position.

This exercise benefits digestion, excretion and reproductive systems. It stretches the stomach and intestine, helps constipation, lumbago, rounded back and backache.

Energizing the Blue Centre

Most of us have tension in the shoulders and need some kind of exercise that presses the chin in and out. But unless he has a very bad neck, a thin person with an already over-active thyroid should avoid these exercises, which may aggravate the problem.

1. Lie flat on the stomach. Extend the hands in front and stretch well. Place the hands in front of the face under the chin, palms one on top of the other. Come up a little with the help of the hands and stretch. Then raise the body without the hands by lifting the hands and elbows along with the chin. When you have risen to the highest point at which you can hold the position without dropping again, bring the elbows into the side of the body allowing the hands to come back to the ground without lowering the body. Lower the head so the back of the neck is fully stretched and bring the body back to the ground with the top of the forehead on the mat. Now, on the in-breath raise the head and hands together as high as the hands will allow, and then, in order to come up higher, put the hands back on to the ground and push up again. Do not lift the base of the stomach off the ground and do not straighten the elbows until you are capable of bending well back. Come down slowly on the out-breath, holding the chin up and hissing to prevent a quick release of the out-breath.

The blue throat centre is boosted in this exercise, but it is often better to concentrate on the forehead so the indigo centre is boosted too. This exercise helps to strengthen the back and abdomen.

For variation, when you have come up to the highest point with the head back, instead of hissing down, just drop the head and breathe out. Then turn the head slowly round to the right and look at the heels with the corner of the eyes on the in-breath. Bring the head back to the centre on the out-breath. Repeat on the other side.

A further variation is to move down on the right elbow and look round and up at the ceiling on the in-breath. On the out-breath, come up and bring the head down. Repeat on the other side.

2. Lie down on the back with the feet together and arms by the sides. Place the palms flat on the ground and use them with the bent elbows and arms to raise the legs up and back into a vertical position. Place the palms as high up the back as possible for support. Press the chin against the chest. Clench the buttock muscles to keep the back as high and straight as possible. This shoulder stand is a very potent exercise but do not attempt it if you have an enlarged thyroid or high blood-pressure, nor when menstruating. When coming down from this reversed position do not stand up straight away. Allow the head to settle a little.

Once you achieve this position, enjoy these variations. They are less effective for the throat centre but make the body more mobile.

Once in the shoulder stand:

a. Allow one leg to come down slowly behind the head. Repeat the other side.

b. Bend the leg at the knee and put it on the forehead, placing the
   foot of that leg on the left knee. Hold for a few moments and
   repeat on the other side.

c. Bring both feet behind on to the floor. Stretch the hands forward holding the wrist if possible.

3. Down from the shoulder stand, bring the feet in until the heels are close to the buttocks and with the legs bent, raise the buttocks up until the chin presses down to the chest. Arch the back, keeping feet and shoulders flat on the floor and support the body with the feet, neck, shoulders and arms.

This exercise helps round shoulders and backache but should not be attempted during pregnancy.

For variation, try to straighten the legs in that position. Supporting your hips with the hands, lift one leg at a time.

4. Here we bring in a few standing exercises. The earlier backbend exercise while kneeling energized the heart centre. Backbend exercises while standing energize the throat centre too. The further back you can bend, the more supple you are, the more the effect ripples through all the centres.

Stand with feet slight apart. On the in-breath, stretch up as high as possible. On the out-breath bend slowly back, pushing the hips and knees forward to counter-balance. Arch backwards as much as possible and stretch well. Come back slowly on the in-breath and drop gently forward on another out-breath.

5. Stand with the feet about a yard apart, pointing slightly to the sides. Bring your hands round to the back and interlock the fingers. Breathe in and stretch the body upwards. Breathe out and bend forward on to one knee, raising the arms behind. Bring the nose as close as possible to the knee and hold for a short time. Slowly lower the arms and repeat on the other side.

This exercise strengthens the muscles between the upper spine and shoulder blades.

Energizing the Indigo Centre

The effectiveness of the forehead depends on the muscles of the face
and head being in tune. The structure needs to be mobile and facial
exercise is important. We are working upwards towards awareness and
you will notice, for example, that animals, when they are aware, prick
back their ears. After the age of twenty, human ears and eyebrows
drop.

These exercises which are also an excellent beauty routine, should be
done every day, three or four times each. Head rotations and clenching
of facial muscles may, however, increase an already over-active thyroid
and should be avoided by thin people.

1. Rub the hands together to energize them. Place the heels of the
hands close together above the eyebrows and put the fingers on to the
top of the head. Concentrate on the whole area. There is a muscle
beneath the hair which pulls the forehead up, and the idea is to contract
this muscle up and back. Do this by tilting the head forward and then
lifting and looking up on the out-breath. If possible hold for a count of
six and drop the head down on the out-breath.

This exercise will decrease wrinkles on the forehead as well as allow
the area to function more effectively.

2. Take the heel of one hand and place between the eyebrows. Press
down on the in-breath and contract the eyebrows for a few moments.
Release on the out-breath. This will activate the muscles at the back of
the head and those around the eyes.

3. Place the heels of the hands over the ears. Beneath each temple is a
strong muscle that lifts the skin at the sides of the face and ears.
Contract this muscle by pulling up the ears on the in-breath and
holding for a few moments. Release on the out-breath.

4. Behind the ears are muscles which pull the ears back. Put the finger tips behind the ears and on the in-breath pull back the ears making them contract. Release on the out-breath.

5. Put the hands at the back of the neck where the hairline ends, fingers about one inch apart. Beneath the scalp at the back of the head is a sheath of muscles. Contract these by pulling the scalp towards the fingertips on the in-breath, moving the fingers towards each other. Relax by opening the fingers and stroking the neck.

6. Rub the hands together once more and place the heels of the hands around the boney structure of the eyes. Tilt the head and lift it up and back on the in-breath and look up. Hold for a few moments. As you look up the first time concentrate on the centre of the forehead; then consecutively on the beginning, centre and ends of the eyebrows. When you release bring the head down, close the eyes, cap them with your hands and relax.

7. Pull the lips together as though to whistle or kiss a few times. Then open the mouth as wide as possible.

8. Tilt the head back. Open and shut the mouth four or five times, clenching the jaw. Then clench the lower lip over the upper lip several times.

9. Drop the head forward, tilt it to one side and rotate very slowly round. Either take an in-breath all the way round or take an in-breath in to the back and an out-breath coming forward. Do this two or three times, one side then the other.

10. Place the fingertips on the shoulders. On the in-breath lift the elbows forward and bend the head forward into a circling movement. On the out-breath bring the head up and the elbows down.

Energizing the Violet Centre

Unless we are able to transmit cosmic energies naturally, we must push
the circulation of blood towards the head to activate the crown centre
and utilise the brain more fully. If we can also put the feet on the head,
the area is activated further. In the ancient days, the whole body was
turned upside down, but unless we have perfect posture (which is
rarely the case), these exercises should be avoided. The following
exercises should be attempted only after you have practised yoga for
some time and only under the guidance of a teacher, although any
exercise in which we bend forward is helpful towards this. Remember,
in all exercises in which the body is reversed, you should not bring the
head up straight away. After pressure on the crown, the head should be
kept down for a few seconds.

1. Stand with the legs three or four feet apart. Take an in-breath.
Turn the body to the right and on the out-breath bring the hands down
slowly, bending the knee and lowering the head as far as possible
towards the ground. Bring the hands inside the right knee to support
the body. Breathe in and come up. Repeat on the other side.

Then move into the centre. On the out-breath bend at the hips and come down in the middle, placing the hands directly in front of the feet. Drop the crown of the head as close as possible between the hands.

Vary this by joining the fingers on the back of the head, or fold the arms in front of the head and go down once more on the out-breath. Stay a little longer in the pose if you wish, breathing normally.

A further variation is to raise the arms and place them in a prayer position on the back. Balance on the head and feet for a few minutes and then return on the in breath.

This pose should not be attempted by people with high blood-pressure or vertigo.

2. Kneel down. Open out the hands, keeping the knees together. Place the top of the head down and come up on the toes at the back. Slowly lift the knees to give a small boost. Hold for a few minutes.

From this position, come down on the knees to rest, then come up again, walking the feet towards the elbows and prop the knees on the elbows to make a tripod on which to rest.

3. Once this position is easily held, rise up to the supported head stand. Remain for a comfortable period and slowly return by refolding the legs and lowering the toes to the ground.

4. Kneel. Bend forward and place the forearms in front of the knees. Move the elbows apart a little. Link the fingers and place the head with the apex on the ground, firmly into the hands. Raise the knees off the ground, and walk the legs towards the trunk until the back becomes straight and thighs press against the abdomen and lower chest. Transfer the body weight from the toes to the head and arms. Raise one foot a little from the ground and then the other. When perfectly balanced, slowly raise and straighten the hips, knees and legs until the body is straight. Maintain the final position for as long as it feels comfortable and then slowly refold the legs and place the toes on to the ground. Rest well before standing. Beginners should only attempt this exercise at the end of an exercise session and only remain inverted for about half a minute. Gradually increase the time up to five minutes.

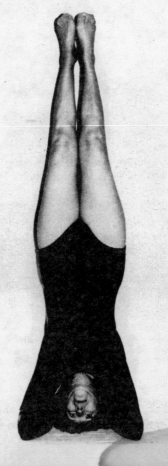

5. Lie flat on the stomach. Extend the hands in front and stretch well. Place the hands in front of the face under the chin, palms one on top of the other. Come up a little with the help of the hands and stretch. Then raise the body without the hands by lifting the hands and elbows along with the chin. When you have risen to the highest point at which you can hold the position without dropping back again, bring the elbows into the sides of the body allowing the hands to come back to the ground without lowering the body. Lower the head so the back of the neck is fully stretched, and bring the body back to the ground with the top of the forehead on the mat. Now, on the in-breath, pushing with the hands, raise the head as high as possible, at the same time bring the feet up from the back, as near as possible to the head. Hold for a few moments and relax on the out-breath.

This highly symbolic exercise represents the ancient vision of unity in which the snake eats its tail. The energies from the feet reach the top of the head, creating the perfect exchange.

Of further interest . . .

WHAT NUMBER ARE YOU?

Your Numbers and Your Life

Lilla Bek & Robert Holden

Your birthdate, your birthplace and your name each have their own individual numbers. So too has each year, each month and each day of your life. *What Number Are You?* translates the language of numbers. It helps you to identify the essential numbers in your life and tells you exactly what these numbers may mean to you.

The study of numbers is an exciting exploration and adventure into an ancient tradition of personal development and self-realization. The ultimate aim of numerology is to fit in, to synchronise and to make peace – with both the world around us and the world within us. This is numerology.

1 85538 135 4 £5.99